Introduction to Tornado

Michael Dory, Adam Parrish, and Brendan Berg

O'REILLY®

Beijing · Cambridge · Farnham · Köln · Sebastopol · Tokyo

Introduction to Tornado

by Michael Dory, Adam Parrish, and Brendan Berg

Published by O'Reilly Media, Inc., 1005 Gravenstein Highway North, Sebastopol, CA 95472.

O'Reilly books may be purchased for educational, business, or sales promotional use. Online editions are also available for most titles (*http://my.safaribooksonline.com*). For more information, contact our corporate/institutional sales department: (800) 998-9938 or *corporate@oreilly.com*.

Editors: Andy Oram and Mike Hendrickson	**Cover Designer:** Karen Montgomery
Production Editor: Melanie Yarbrough	**Interior Designer:** David Futato
	Illustrator: Robert Romano

Revision History for the First Edition:

2012-03-16   First release
See *http://oreilly.com/catalog/errata.csp?isbn=9781449309077* for release details.

ISBN: 978-1-449-30907-7

[LSI]

1331730489

Table of Contents

Preface

Conventions Used in This Book

The following typographical conventions are used in this book:

Italic

Indicates new terms, URLs, email addresses, filenames, and file extensions.

`Constant width`

Used for program listings, as well as within paragraphs to refer to program elements such as variable or function names, databases, data types, environment variables, statements, and keywords.

`Constant width bold`

Shows commands or other text that should be typed literally by the user.

`Constant width italic`

Shows text that should be replaced with user-supplied values or by values determined by context.

> This icon signifies a tip, suggestion, or general note.

> This icon indicates a warning or caution.

Using Code Examples

This book is here to help you get your job done. In general, you may use the code in this book in your programs and documentation. You do not need to contact us for permission unless you're reproducing a significant portion of the code. For example, writing a program that uses several chunks of code from this book does not require permission. Selling or distributing a CD-ROM of examples from O'Reilly books does require permission. Answering a question by citing this book and quoting example code does not require permission. Incorporating a significant amount of example code from this book into your product's documentation does require permission.

We appreciate, but do not require, attribution. An attribution usually includes the title, author, publisher, and ISBN. For example: "*Introduction to Tornado* by Michael Dory, Adam Parrish, and Brendan Berg (O'Reilly). Copyright 2012 Michael Dory, Adam Parrish, and Brendan Berg, ISBN 978-1-4493-0907-7."

If you feel your use of code examples falls outside fair use or the permission given above, feel free to contact us at *permissions@oreilly.com*.

Safari® Books Online

Safari Books Online is an on-demand digital library that lets you easily search over 7,500 technology and creative reference books and videos to find the answers you need quickly.

With a subscription, you can read any page and watch any video from our library online. Read books on your cell phone and mobile devices. Access new titles before they are available for print, and get exclusive access to manuscripts in development and post feedback for the authors. Copy and paste code samples, organize your favorites, download chapters, bookmark key sections, create notes, print out pages, and benefit from tons of other time-saving features.

O'Reilly Media has uploaded this book to the Safari Books Online service. To have full digital access to this book and others on similar topics from O'Reilly and other publishers, sign up for free at *http://my.safaribooksonline.com*.

How to Contact Us

Please address comments and questions concerning this book to the publisher:

> O'Reilly Media, Inc.
> 1005 Gravenstein Highway North
> Sebastopol, CA 95472
> 800-998-9938 (in the United States or Canada)
> 707-829-0515 (international or local)
> 707-829-0104 (fax)

We have a web page for this book, where we list errata, examples, and any additional information. You can access this page at:

> *http://shop.oreilly.com/product/0636920021292.do*

To comment or ask technical questions about this book, send email to:

> *bookquestions@oreilly.com*

For more information about our books, courses, conferences, and news, see our website at *http://www.oreilly.com*.

Find us on Facebook: *http://facebook.com/oreilly*

Follow us on Twitter: *http://twitter.com/oreillymedia*

Watch us on YouTube: *http://www.youtube.com/oreillymedia*

Acknowledgements

We'd like to thank our editor Andy Oram, for all his guidance and insight as we wrote and edited this book, and the O'Reilly community at large for being so helpful and supportive as we went. What started as a short submission to OSCon ultimately led to a host of great things, not least of which is the opportunity to write this book, and we're thrilled to have had the chance to do it.

We'd like to give tremendous thanks to Sumana Harihareswara, who convinced us to start talking about Tornado in the first place, and to Socialbomb and Wurk Happy for giving us the support and opportunity to tinker, explore, and experiment, and eventually prescribe, advocate, and rely on this great software.

Further, we could not have made this book half of what it is without the amazing reviewers who shared their thoughts and opinions with us. The feedback from Jeff Gray, James Linder, Randy Jimenez, and Jonathan Bourland all helped mold our final product.

Witnessing the community that develops around open source projects is particularly inspiring. Seeing Tornado take root so quickly is a testament to Bret Taylor and Dave Recordon's foresight and skill. We would like to thank them, and all the developers whose contributions to Tornado have given us something worth writing about.

Finally, this book could not have been created without the atmosphere, WiFi, and caffeine supply of the coffeehouses of Brooklyn, Manhattan, and Jersey City, to whom we are forever indebted.

Mike would like to express his eternal gratitude to his family and friends for their constant support and encouragement, especially to Jean and John Dory, who understood that a love of blinky lights and black coffee might turn into something useful after all. A big thanks is due to the NYU ITP alumni, faculty, and staff that serve as a constant feed of guidance, support, and ever-evolving inspiration. And most importantly, to his wife Rita, whose encouragement, advice, and understanding made this and everything else possible.

Adam is indebted to his students at NYU's Interactive Telecommunications Program, for whom much of the material in early chapters of the book was originally prepared. Their enthusiasm for the material proved that a book like this one would have an audience, and their helpful feedback made the book better.

Brendan would have had neither the interest, the inclination, nor the aptitude to embark on this project without the 128K Mac that lived in the office on the third floor. The ember that leaped from that little beige box was tended along the way by his parents, Bruce and Catie, and by innumerable mentors and teachers along the way. Thanks especially to Tom Roney and Bob McGrail, who inspired a deep understanding of computation, software, and systems.

CHAPTER 1
Introduction

Over the last half decade, the tools available to web developers have grown by leaps and bounds. As technologists continue to push the limits of what web applications can do for users everywhere, we've had to upgrade our toolkit and create frameworks that let us build better applications. We would like to be able to use new toolkits that make it easier for us to write clean and maintainable code that scales efficiently when deployed to users all across the globe.

This brings us to talking about Tornado, a fantastic choice for writing powerful web applications that are simple to create, extend, and deploy. The three of us had all fallen in love with Tornado for its speed, simplicity, and scalability, and after trying it out on a few personal projects, we've put it to work in our day jobs. We've seen it increase developer speed (and happiness!) on projects large and small, and at the same time have been impressed time and again by its robustness and lightweight footprint.

This book is meant to be an overview of the Tornado web server, and will walk readers through the basics of the framework, some sample applications, and best practices for use in the real world. We'll use examples to detail how Tornado works, what you can do with it, and what you'd be best avoiding as you build your first applications with it.

In this book, we'll be assuming that you have at least a rough understanding of Python, a sense of how web services work, and a basic familiarity with databases. For more on any of those, there are some great books to consult (including *Learning Python*, *Restful Web Services*, and *MongoDB: The Definitive Guide*).

And so you can follow along, the code for the examples in this book is available on Github (*https://github.com/Introduction-to-Tornado*). If you have any thoughts on these samples or anything else, we'd love to hear from you there.

So, without further ado, let's dive in!

What Is Tornado?

Tornado is a powerful, scalable web server written in Python. It's robust enough to handle serious web traffic, yet is lightweight to set up and write for, and can be used for a variety of applications and utilities.

The Tornado we now know is based on a web server framework that was first developed by Bret Taylor and others for FriendFeed, and later open sourced by Facebook when they acquired FriendFeed. Unlike traditional web servers that maxed out at around 10,000 simultaneous connections, Tornado was written with performance in mind, aiming to solve the C10K problem, so by design it's an extremely high-performance framework. It's also packed with tools for dealing with security and user authentication, social networks, and asynchronous interaction with external services like databases and web APIs.

A Bit More About the C10K Problem

Thread-based servers like Apache maintain a pool of OS threads for incoming connections. Apache assigns each HTTP connection to one of those threads, spawning a new thread if all existing threads are busy and more memory is available. Although it varies from system to system, most Linux distributions have an 8 MB default thread stack size. Apache's architecture scales unpredictably under load, and maintaining a large pool of open connections that are each waiting for data can easily consume all the free memory available to a server.

Most social web applications display real-time updates for new messages, status changes, and user notifications, which require the client keep an open connection waiting for any server responses. These HTTP keep-alive or Comet requests can quickly saturate Apache's maximum thread pool. Once the thread pool is depleted of available workers, the server is unable to respond to new requests.

Asynchronous servers are relatively new to the scene, but they are designed to alleviate the limitations of thread-based web servers. Servers such as Node.js, lighttpd, and Tornado use cooperative multitasking to scale gracefully as load increases. That is to say, an asynchronous server will explicitly yield control to pending requests if the current request is waiting for data from another source (a database query or HTTP request, for example). A common pattern that asynchronous servers use to resume a paused operation is to invoke callbacks when the appropriate data is ready. We discuss the callback pattern and a number of applications for Tornado's asynchronous features in Chapter 5.

Since its release on September 10, 2009, Tornado has garnered a lot of community support, and has been adopted to fit a variety of purposes. In addition to FriendFeed and Facebook, a host of companies have turned to Tornado in production, including Quora, Turntable.fm, Bit.ly, Hipmunk, and MyYearbook, to name a few.

In short, if you're looking for a replacement for your giant CMS or monolithic development framework, Tornado is probably not the way to go. Tornado doesn't require that you have giant models set up a particular way, or handle forms in a certain fashion, or anything like that. What it *does* do is let you write super fast web applications quickly and easily. If you want to create a scalable social application, real-time analytics engine, or RESTful API—all with the power and simplicity of Python—then Tornado (and this book) is for you!

Getting Started with Tornado

Installing Tornado on most *nix systems is easy—you can either get it from PyPI (and install via `easy_install` or `pip`), or download the source from Github and build it like this:

```
$ curl -L -O http://github.com/downloads/facebook/tornado/tornado-2.1.1.tar.gz
$ tar xvzf tornado-2.1.1.tar.gz
$ cd tornado-2.1.1
$ python setup.py build
$ sudo python setup.py install
```

Tornado is not officially supported on Windows, but it can be installed via ActivePython's PyPM package manager like so:

```
C:\> pypm install tornado
```

Once Tornado is installed on your machine, you're good to go! A bunch of demos are included with the package, which include examples for building a blog, integrating with Facebook, running a chat server, and more. We'll be walking through some sample applications step by step later in this book, but be sure to have a look at these later for reference as well.

 We're assuming for these examples that you are using a Unix-based system and have Python 2.6 or 2.7 installed. If so, you won't need anything aside from the Python standard library. You can run Tornado under Python 2.5 provided you have installed `pycURL`, `simpleJSON`, and the Python development headers, and on Python 3.2 with the `distribute` package. However, you should note that Python 3+ support is new as of Tornado 2.0, and the Tornado team has advised developers to continue to keep an eye out for bugs on that front.

Community and Support

For questions, examples, and general how-to's, the official Tornado documentation is a great place to start. There's a variety of examples and breakdowns of features at tornadoweb.org (*http://tornadoweb.org*), and more specific details and changes can be seen at Facebook's Tornado repository on Github (*http://github.com/facebook/tornado*). For more specific concerns, the Tornado Web Server Google Group (*http://*

groups.google.com/group/python-tornado) is active and full of folks who use Tornado on a daily basis.

Simple Web Services

Now that we've covered what Tornado is, let's look at what it can do. To start, we'll go over the basics of writing a simple web service with Tornado.

Hello Tornado

Tornado is a framework for writing responses to HTTP requests. Your job as a programmer is to write "handlers" that respond to HTTP requests that match particular criteria. Here's a basic example of a fully functional Tornado application:

Example 1-1. The basics: hello.py

```
import tornado.httpserver
import tornado.ioloop
import tornado.options
import tornado.web

from tornado.options import define, options
define("port", default=8000, help="run on the given port", type=int)

class IndexHandler(tornado.web.RequestHandler):
    def get(self):
        greeting = self.get_argument('greeting', 'Hello')
        self.write(greeting + ', friendly user!')

if __name__ == "__main__":
    tornado.options.parse_command_line()
    app = tornado.web.Application(handlers=[(r"/", IndexHandler)])
    http_server = tornado.httpserver.HTTPServer(app)
    http_server.listen(options.port)
    tornado.ioloop.IOLoop.instance().start()
```

Most of the work in making a Tornado application is to define classes that extend the Tornado `RequestHandler` class. In this case, we've made a simple application that listens for requests on a given port, and responds to requests to the root resource ("/").

Try running the program yourself on the command line to test it out:

```
$ python hello.py --port=8000
```

Now you can go to `http://localhost:8000/` in a web browser, or open up a separate terminal window to test out the application with curl:

```
$ curl http://localhost:8000/
Hello, friendly user!
$ curl http://localhost:8000/?greeting=Salutations
Salutations, friendly user!
```

Let's break this example down into smaller chunks and analyze them one by one:

```
import tornado.httpserver
import tornado.ioloop
import tornado.options
import tornado.web
```

At the top of the program, we import various Tornado libraries. There are other helpful libraries included with Tornado, but you'll need to import at least these four to get this example running:

```
from tornado.options import define, options
define("port", default=8000, help="run on the given port", type=int)
```

Tornado includes a helpful library (`tornado.options`) for reading options from the command line. We make use of that library here to let us specify which port our application will listen on for HTTP requests. Here's how it works: any option in a `define` statement will become available as an attribute of the global `options` object, if an option with the same name is given on the command line. If the user runs the program with the `--help` parameter, the program will print out all of the options you've defined, along with the text you specified with the `help` parameter in the call to `define`. If the user fails to provide a value for an option we specified, the `default` value for that option will be used instead. Tornado uses the `type` parameter to do basic type checking on the parameter, throwing an error if a value of an inappropriate type is given. Our line, therefore, allows the user to use an integer `port` argument, which we can access in the body of the program as `options.port`. If the user doesn't specify a value, it defaults to `8000`.

```
class IndexHandler(tornado.web.RequestHandler):
    def get(self):
        greeting = self.get_argument('greeting', 'Hello')
        self.write(greeting + ', friendly user!')
```

This is a Tornado request handler class. When handling a request, Tornado instantiates this class and calls the method corresponding to the HTTP method of the request. In this example, we've defined only a `get` method, meaning that this handler will respond only to HTTP GET requests. We'll look at handlers that implement more than one HTTP method later.

```
greeting = self.get_argument('greeting', 'Hello')
```

Tornado's `RequestHandler` class has a number of useful built-in methods, including `get_argument`, which we use here to get an argument `greeting` from the query string. (If no such argument is present in the query string, Tornado will use the second argument provided to `get_argument`, if any, as a default.)

```
self.write(greeting + ', friendly user!')
```

Another method of the `RequestHandler` class is `write`, which takes a string as a parameter and writes that string into the HTTP response. Here, we take the string supplied in the request's greeting parameter, interpolate it into a greeting, and write it back in the response.

```
if __name__ == "__main__":
    tornado.options.parse_command_line()
    app = tornado.web.Application(handlers=[(r"/", IndexHandler)])
```

These are the lines that actually make the Tornado application run. First, we use Tornado's options library to parse the command line. Then we create an instance of Tornado's Application class. The most important argument to pass to the __init__ method of the Application class is handlers. This tells Tornado which classes to use to handle which requests. More on this in a moment.

```
http_server = tornado.httpserver.HTTPServer(app)
http_server.listen(options.port)
tornado.ioloop.IOLoop.instance().start()
```

From here on out, this code is boilerplate: once it has been created, we can pass the Application object to Tornado's HTTPServer object, which then listens to the port we specified on the command line (retrieved through the options object). Finally, we create an instance of Tornado's IOLoop, after which point the program is ready to accept HTTP requests.

The handlers Parameter

Let's take a look at one line from the *hello.py* example again:

```
app = tornado.web.Application(handlers=[(r"/", IndexHandler)])
```

The handlers parameter here is important, and worth looking at in further detail. It should be a list of tuples, with each tuple containing a regular expression to match as its first member and a RequestHandler class as its second member. In hello.py, we specified only one regular expression RequestHandler pair, but you can put as many of these pairs into the list as needed.

Specifying paths with regular expressions

Tornado uses the regular expression in the tuples to match the *path* of the HTTP request. (The path is the portion of the URL that follows the hostname, excluding the query string and fragment.) Tornado treats these regular expressions as though they contain beginning-of-line and end-of-line anchors (i.e., the string "/" is assumed to mean "^/$").

When a regular expression has a capture group in it (i.e., a portion of the regular expression is enclosed in parentheses), the matching contents of that group will be passed to the RequestHandler object as parameters to the method corresponding to the HTTP request. We'll see how this works in the next example.

String Service

Example 1-2 is a more sophisticated example program that illustrates what we've gone over so far and introduces a few more basic Tornado concepts.

Example 1-2. Handling input: string_service.py

```python
import textwrap

import tornado.httpserver
import tornado.ioloop
import tornado.options
import tornado.web

from tornado.options import define, options
define("port", default=8000, help="run on the given port", type=int)

class ReverseHandler(tornado.web.RequestHandler):
    def get(self, input):
        self.write(input[::-1])

class WrapHandler(tornado.web.RequestHandler):
    def post(self):
        text = self.get_argument('text')
        width = self.get_argument('width', 40)
        self.write(textwrap.fill(text, width))

if __name__ == "__main__":
    tornado.options.parse_command_line()
    app = tornado.web.Application(
        handlers=[
            (r"/reverse/(\w+)", ReverseHandler),
            (r"/wrap", WrapHandler)
        ]
    )
    http_server = tornado.httpserver.HTTPServer(app)
    http_server.listen(options.port)
    tornado.ioloop.IOLoop.instance().start()
```

As with the first example, you can run this program on the command line by typing the following:

```
$ python string_service.py --port=8000
```

The program is a basic framework for an all-purpose web service for string manipulation. Right now, you can do two things with it. First, GET requests to /reverse/**string** returns the string specified in the URL path in reverse:

```
$ curl http://localhost:8000/reverse/stressed
desserts

$ curl http://localhost:8000/reverse/slipup
pupils
```

Second, POST requests to the /wrap resource will take text specified in an argument text and return that text, wrapped to the width specified in an argument named width. The following request specifies a string but no width, so the output is wrapped to the default width specified in the program's get_argument call, 40 characters:

```
$ curl http://localhost:8000/wrap »
-d text=Lorem+ipsum+dolor+sit+amet,+consectetuer+adipiscing+elit.
Lorem ipsum dolor sit amet, consectetuer
adipiscing elit.
```

 The cURL command just shown was broken onto two lines for formatting reasons, but should be typed as a single line. As a convention, we will use the right double quote character (») to indicate a line continuation.

The string service example shares most of its code with the example presented in the previous section. Let's zero in on some parts of the code that are new. First, let's look at the value passed in the handlers parameter to the Application constructor:

```
app = tornado.web.Application(handlers=[
    (r"/reverse/(\w+)", ReverseHandler),
    (r"/wrap", WrapHandler)
])
```

In the previous code, the Application class is instantiated with two RequestHandlers in the "handlers" parameter. The first directs Tornado to send requests whose path matches the following regular expression:

```
/reverse/(\w+)
```

This regular expression tells Tornado to match any path beginning with the string /reverse/ followed by one or more alphanumeric characters. The parentheses tell Tornado to save the string that matched inside the parentheses, and pass that string to the RequestHandler's request method as a parameter. Check out the definition of ReverseHandler to see how it works:

```
class ReverseHandler(tornado.web.RequestHandler):
    def get(self, input):
        self.write(input[::-1])
```

You can see here that the get method takes an additional parameter input. This parameter will contain whatever string was matched inside the first set of parentheses in the regular expression that matched the handler. (If there are additional sets of parentheses in the regular expression, the matched strings will be passed in as additional parameters, in the same order as they occurred in the regular expression.)

Now, let's take a look at the definition of WrapHandler:

```
class WrapHandler(tornado.web.RequestHandler):
    def post(self):
        text = self.get_argument('text')
```

```
    width = self.get_argument('width', 40)
    self.write(textwrap.fill(text, width))
```

The WrapHandler class handles requests that match the path /wrap. This handler defines a post method, meaning that it accepts requests with an HTTP method of POST.

We've previously used the RequestHandler object's get_argument method to grab parameters off of a request's query string. It turns out we can use the same method to get parameters passed into a POST request. (Tornado understands POST requests with URL-encoded or multipart bodies.) Once we've grabbed the text and width arguments from the POST body, we use Python's built-in textwrap library to wrap the text to the specified width, and write the resulting string to the HTTP response.

More About RequestHandlers

So far, we've explored the bare basics of RequestHandler objects: how to get information from an incoming HTTP request (using get_argument and the parameters passed to get and post) and how to write an HTTP response (using the write method). There's a lot more to learn, which we'll get to in subsequent chapters. In the meantime, here are a few things to keep in mind about RequestHandler and how Tornado uses it.

HTTP methods

In the examples discussed so far, each RequestHandler class has defined behavior for only one HTTP method. However, it's possible—and useful—to define multiple methods in the same handler. This is a good way to keep conceptually related functionality bundled into the same class. For example, you might write one handler for both a GET and a POST to an object in a database with a particular ID. Here's an imaginary example, in which the GET method for a widget ID returns information about that widget, and the POST method makes changes to the widget with that ID in the database:

```
# matched with (r"/widget/(\d+)", WidgetHandler)
class WidgetHandler(tornado.web.RequestHandler):
    def get(self, widget_id):
        widget = retrieve_from_db(widget_id)
        self.write(widget.serialize())

    def post(self, widget_id):
        widget = retrieve_from_db(widget_id)
        widget['foo'] = self.get_argument('foo')
        save_to_db(widget)
```

We've used only GET and POST in our examples so far, but Tornado supports any valid HTTP method (GET, POST, PUT, DELETE, HEAD, OPTIONS). You can define behavior for any of these methods simply by defining a method in your RequestHandler class with a matching name. The following is another imaginary example, in which a HEAD request for a particular frob ID gives information only concerning whether or not the frob exists, while the GET method returns the full object:

```
# matched with (r"/frob/(\d+)", FrobHandler)
class FrobHandler(tornado.web.RequestHandler):
    def head(self, frob_id):
        frob = retrieve_from_db(frob_id)
        if frob is not None:
            self.set_status(200)
        else:
            self.set_status(404)
    def get(self, frob_id):
        frob = retrieve_from_db(frob_id)
        self.write(frob.serialize())
```

HTTP status codes

As shown in the previous example, you can explicitly set the HTTP status code of your response by calling the `set_status()` method of the `RequestHandler`. It's important to note, however, that Tornado will set the HTTP status code of your response automatically under some circumstances. Here's a rundown of the most common cases:

404 Not Found

> Tornado will automatically return a 404 (Not Found) response code if the path of the HTTP request doesn't match any pattern associated with a `RequestHandler` class.

400 Bad Request

> If you call `get_argument` without a default, and no argument with the given name is found, Tornado will automatically return a 400 (Bad Request) response code.

405 Method Not Allowed

> If an incoming request uses an HTTP method that the matching `RequestHandler` doesn't define (e.g., the request is `POST` but the handler class only defines a `get` method), Tornado will return a 405 (Method Not Allowed) response code.

500 Internal Server Error

> Tornado will return 500 (Internal Server Error) when it encounters any errors that aren't severe enough to cause the program to exit. Any uncaught exceptions in your code will also cause Tornado to return a 500 response code.

200 OK

> If the response was successful and no other status code was set, Tornado will return a 200 (OK) response code by default.

When one of the errors above occurs, Tornado will by default send a brief snippet of HTML to the client with the status code and information about the error. If you'd like to replace the default error responses with your own, you can override the `write_error` method in your `RequestHandler` class. For example, Example 1-3 shows our initial *hello.py* example, but with custom error messages.

Example 1-3. Custom error responses: hello-errors.py

```
import tornado.httpserver
import tornado.ioloop
import tornado.options
import tornado.web

from tornado.options import define, options
define("port", default=8000, help="run on the given port", type=int)

class IndexHandler(tornado.web.RequestHandler):
    def get(self):
        greeting = self.get_argument('greeting', 'Hello')
        self.write(greeting + ', friendly user!')
    def write_error(self, status_code, **kwargs):
        self.write("Gosh darnit, user! You caused a %d error." % status_code)

if __name__ == "__main__":
    tornado.options.parse_command_line()
    app = tornado.web.Application(handlers=[(r"/", IndexHandler)])
    http_server = tornado.httpserver.HTTPServer(app)
    http_server.listen(options.port)
    tornado.ioloop.IOLoop.instance().start()
```

The following response is what happens when we attempt to POST to this handler. Normally, we would get Tornado's default error response, but because we've overridden write_error, we get something else:

```
$ curl -d foo=bar http://localhost:8000/
Gosh darnit, user! You caused a 405 error.
```

Next Steps

By now you've got the basics under your belt, and we hope you're hungry for more. In the upcoming chapters, we'll show features and techniques that will help you use Tornado to build full-blown web services and web applications. First up: Tornado's template system.

CHAPTER 2

Forms and Templates

In Chapter 1, we looked at the basics of setting up a web application with Tornado. We covered handlers, HTTP methods, and the overall structure of the Tornado framework. In this chapter, we're going to take a look at some of the more powerful features that you're likely to use when building web applications.

As with most web frameworks, one of the primary goals of Tornado is to help you write your applications faster, reusing as much of your code as cleanly as possible. While Tornado is flexible enough to allow you to use nearly any template language supported by Python, it contains a lightweight, fast, and flexible templating language within the `tornado.template` module.

Simple Example: Poem Maker Pro

Let's get started with a simple example called *Poem Maker Pro*. Poem Maker Pro is a web application that presents an HTML form for the user to fill out, and then processes the results of that form. See Example 2-1 for the Python code.

Example 2-1. Simple forms and templates: poemmaker.py

```
import os.path

import tornado.httpserver
import tornado.ioloop
import tornado.options
import tornado.web

from tornado.options import define, options
define("port", default=8000, help="run on the given port", type=int)

class IndexHandler(tornado.web.RequestHandler):
    def get(self):
        self.render('index.html')

class PoemPageHandler(tornado.web.RequestHandler):
    def post(self):
```

```
        noun1 = self.get_argument('noun1')
        noun2 = self.get_argument('noun2')
        verb = self.get_argument('verb')
        noun3 = self.get_argument('noun3')
        self.render('poem.html', roads=noun1, wood=noun2, made=verb,
                difference=noun3)

if __name__ == '__main__':
    tornado.options.parse_command_line()
    app = tornado.web.Application(
        handlers=[(r'/', IndexHandler), (r'/poem', PoemPageHandler)],
        template_path=os.path.join(os.path.dirname(__file__), "templates")
    )
    http_server = tornado.httpserver.HTTPServer(app)
    http_server.listen(options.port)
    tornado.ioloop.IOLoop.instance().start()
```

In addition to *poemmaker.py*, you'll need the two files shown in Examples 2-2 and 2-3 in a subdirectory called *templates*.

Example 2-2. Poem Maker form: index.html

```
<!DOCTYPE html>
<html>
    <head><title>Poem Maker Pro</title></head>
    <body>
        <h1>Enter terms below.</h1>
        <form method="post" action="/poem">
        <p>Plural noun<br><input type="text" name="noun1"></p>
        <p>Singular noun<br><input type="text" name="noun2"></p>
        <p>Verb (past tense)<br><input type="text" name="verb"></p>
        <p>Noun<br><input type="text" name="noun3"></p>
        <input type="submit">
        </form>
    </body>
</html>
```

Example 2-3. Poem Maker template: poem.html

```
<!DOCTYPE html>
<html>
    <head><title>Poem Maker Pro</title></head>
    <body>
        <h1>Your poem</h1>
        <p>Two {{roads}} diverged in a {{wood}}, and I&mdash;<br>
I took the one less travelled by,<br>
And that has {{made}} all the {{difference}}.</p>
    </body>
</html>
```

Run this program on the command line like so:

```
$ python poemmaker.py --port=8000
```

Now, point your web browser to `http://localhost:8000`. When the web browser requests the root resource (/), the Tornado program will render *index.html*, displaying the simple HTML form in Figure 2-1.

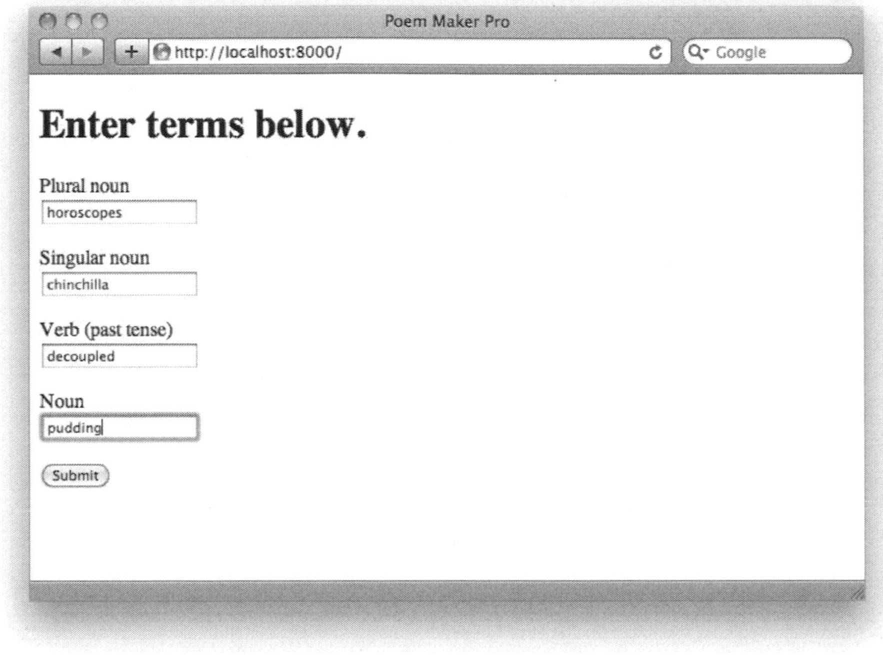

Figure 2-1. Poem Maker Pro: Input form

This form contains a number of text fields (named `noun1`, `noun2`, etc.) whose contents will be sent to `/poem` in a `POST` request when the user clicks the "Submit" button. Now fill in the fields and click Submit.

In response to that `POST` request, the Tornado application rendered *poem.html*, interpolating the values that you typed into the form. The result is a slightly modified version of a stanza of Robert Frost's "The Road Not Taken." Figure 2-2 shows what it looks like.

Rendering Templates

Structurally, `poemmaker.py` is similar to the examples in Chapter 1. We define a few `RequestHandlers` and hand them off to a `tornado.web.Application` object. So what's different? First of all, we're passing the `template_path` parameter to the `__init__` method of the `Application` object:

```
template_path=os.path.join(os.path.dirname(__file__), "templates")
```

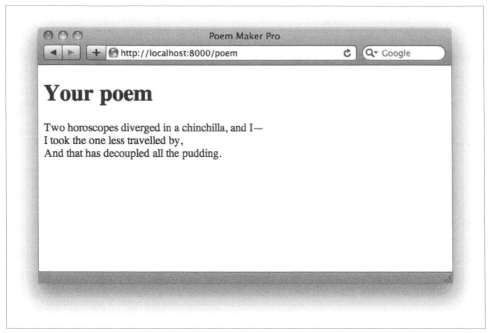

Figure 2-2. Poem Maker Pro: Output

The `template_path` parameter tells Tornado where to look for *template files*. We'll be going into the exact nature and syntax of template files in this chapter and Chapter 3, but the basic gist is this: templates are HTML files that allow you to embed snippets of Python code. The previous code tells Python to look for template files in a directory named *templates*, located in the same directory as your Tornado application file.

Once we've told Tornado where to find templates, we can use the `render` method of the `RequestHandler` class to tell Tornado to read in a template file, interpolate any template code found within, and then send the results to the browser. In `IndexHandler`, for example, we find the following:

```
self.render('index.html')
```

This code will cause Tornado to find a file called *index.html* in the *templates* directory, read its contents, and send it to the browser.

Interpolation

It turns out that *index.html* is hardly a "template" at all, seeing that it consists entirely of prebaked HTML markup. This is a fine use for templates, but more often we'll want the HTML output to incorporate values passed into the template from our program. The *poem.html* template, as rendered by `PoemPageHandler`, is a good example of this. Let's take a look at how it works.

In *poem.html*, you can see several strings enclosed in double curly brackets ({{ and }}) in the template, like so:

```
<p>Two {{roads}} diverged in a {{wood}}, and I&mdash;<br/>
I took the one less travelled by,<br>
And that has {{made}} all the {{difference}}.</p>
```

The words enclosed in double curly brackets are placeholders, which we want to replace with real values when the template is rendered. We can specify what values will be interpolated in the HTML in their place by passing keyword arguments to the render function, with the keywords corresponding to names of the placeholders. Here's the relevant part of the code from PoemPageHandler:

```
noun1 = self.get_argument('noun1')
noun2 = self.get_argument('noun2')
verb = self.get_argument('verb')
noun3 = self.get_argument('noun3')
self.render('poem.html', roads=noun1, wood=noun2, made=verb, difference=noun3)
```

Here, we're telling the template to use the variable noun1 (itself taken from the get_argu ment method) as the value for roads in the template, noun2 as the value for wood in the template, and so forth. Assuming that the user typed **pineapples**, **grandfather clock**, **irradiated**, and **supernovae** into the form (in that order), the resulting HTML would look like this:

```
<p>Two pineapples diverged in a grandfather clock, and I&mdash;<br>
I took the one less travelled by,<br>
And that has irradiated all the supernovae.</p>
```

Template Syntax

Now that we've seen a simple example of templates in action, let's go into a bit more detail about how they work. Templates in Tornado are simply text files marked up with Python expressions and control sequences. The syntax of Tornado templates is fairly straightforward and simple. Users familiar with Django, Liquid, or similar frameworks will find a lot of similarities, and should find it easy to pick up.

In "Simple Example: Poem Maker Pro" on page 13, we showed how to use the ren der method in a web application to send HTML to the browser. You can try out the templating system outside of a Tornado application by importing the template module in the Python interpreter, and printing the output directly.

```
>>> from tornado.template import Template
>>> content = Template("<html><body><h1>{{ header }}</h1></body></html>")
>>> print content.generate(header="Welcome!")
<html><body><h1>Welcome!</h1></body></html>
```

Interpolating Expressions

In Example 2-1, we demonstrated the use of double curly braces to interpolate the value of Python variables into a template. It turns out that you can put any Python expression inside double curly braces. Tornado will insert a string containing whatever that expression evaluated to into the output. Here are a few examples of what's possible:

```
>>> from tornado.template import Template
>>> print Template("{{ 1+1 }}").generate()
2
>>> print Template("{{ 'scrambled eggs'[-4:] }}").generate()
eggs
>>> print Template("{{ ', '.join([str(x*x) for x in range(10)]) }}").generate()
0, 1, 4, 9, 16, 25, 36, 49, 64, 81
```

Control Flow Statements

You can also include Python conditionals and loops in your Tornado templates. Control statements are surrounded by {% and %}, and are used in cases like:

```
{% if page is None %}
```

or

```
{% if len(entries) == 3 %}
```

Control statements for the most part work just like the corresponding Python statements, with support for if, for, while, and try. In each of these cases, {% starts a code block and %} ends it.

So this template:

```
<html>
    <head>
        <title>{{ title }}</title>
    </head>
    <body>
        <h1>{{ header }}</h1>
        <ul>
            {% for book in books %}
                <li>{{ book }}</li>
            {% end %}
        </ul>
    </body>
</html>
```

When called by a handler that looks like this:

```
class BookHandler(tornado.web.RequestHandler):
    def get(self):
        self.render(
            "book.html",
            title="Home Page",
            header="Books that are great",
            books=[
```

```
            "Learning Python",
            "Programming Collective Intelligence",
            "Restful Web Services"
        ]
    )
```

Would render the following output:

```
<html>
    <head>
        <title>Home Page</title>
    </head>
    <body>
        <h1>Books that are great</h1>
        <ul>
            <li>Learning Python</li>
            <li>Programming Collective Intelligence</li>
            <li>Restful Web Services</li>
        </ul>
    </body>
</html>
```

One of the best things about Tornado's template language is that, unlike many other Python templating systems, there are no restrictions on what expressions can be used within `if` and `for` blocks. Therefore, you can execute full Python code within your templates.

You can also use `{% set foo = 'bar' %}` to set variables in the middle of control blocks. There's plenty more you can do just within control blocks, but in most cases, you'll be better served by making use of UI modules to do more complex breakdowns for you. We'll take a look at this more in a little bit.

Using Functions Inside Templates

Tornado offers several handy functions by default in all templates. These include:

`escape(s)`

Replaces &, <, and > in string *s* with their corresponding HTML entities.

`url_escape(s)`

Uses `urllib.quote_plus` to replace characters in string *s* with URL-encoded equivalents.

`json_encode(val)`

Encodes *val* as JSON. (Underneath the hood, this is just a call to the `dumps` function in the `json` library. See the relevant documentation for information about what parameters this function accepts and what it returns.)

`squeeze(s)`

Filters string *s*, replacing sequences of more than one whitespace character with a single space.

In Tornado 1.x, templates are not automatically escaped. In Tornado 2.0, template autoescaping is enabled by default (and can be turned off by passing autoescape=None to the Application constructor). Beware of backwards compatibility when migrating from one to the other.

Using a function you've written inside of a template is easy: just pass the name of the function as a template parameter, like any other variable.

```
>>> from tornado.template import Template
>>> def disemvowel(s):
...     return ''.join([x for x in s if x not in 'aeiou'])
...
>>> disemvowel("george")
'grg'
>>> print Template("my name is {{d('mortimer')}}").generate(d=disemvowel)
my name is mrtmr
```

Complete Example: The Alpha Munger

In Example 2-4, we'll put together everything we talked about in this chapter. The application described is called *The Alpha Munger*. The user inputs two texts: a "source" text and a "replacement" text. The application then returns a copy of the "replacement" text in which each word has been replaced by a word from the source text beginning with the same letter. Figure 2-3 shows the form filled out and Figure 2-4 shows the resulting text.

This application consists of four files: *main.py* (the Tornado program), *style.css* (a CSS stylesheet file), *index.html*, and *munged.html* (Tornado templates). Let's look at the code:

Example 2-4. Complete forms and templates: main.py

```
import os.path
import random

import tornado.httpserver
import tornado.ioloop
import tornado.options
import tornado.web

from tornado.options import define, options
define("port", default=8000, help="run on the given port", type=int)

class IndexHandler(tornado.web.RequestHandler):
    def get(self):
        self.render('index.html')

class MungedPageHandler(tornado.web.RequestHandler):
    def map_by_first_letter(self, text):
        mapped = dict()
        for line in text.split('\r\n'):
```

```
            for word in [x for x in line.split(' ') if len(x) > 0]:
                if word[0] not in mapped: mapped[word[0]] = []
                mapped[word[0]].append(word)
        return mapped

    def post(self):
        source_text = self.get_argument('source')
        text_to_change = self.get_argument('change')
        source_map = self.map_by_first_letter(source_text)
        change_lines = text_to_change.split('\r\n')
        self.render('munged.html', source_map=source_map, change_lines=change_lines,
                choice=random.choice)

if __name__ == '__main__':
    tornado.options.parse_command_line()
    app = tornado.web.Application(
        handlers=[(r'/', IndexHandler), (r'/poem', MungedPageHandler)],
        template_path=os.path.join(os.path.dirname(__file__), "templates"),
        static_path=os.path.join(os.path.dirname(__file__), "static"),
        debug=True
    )
    http_server = tornado.httpserver.HTTPServer(app)
    http_server.listen(options.port)
    tornado.ioloop.IOLoop.instance().start()
```

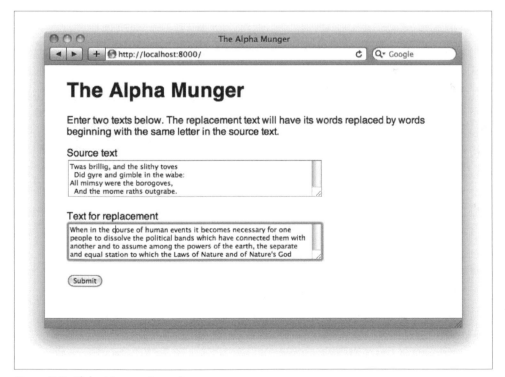

Figure 2-3. Alpha Munger: Input form

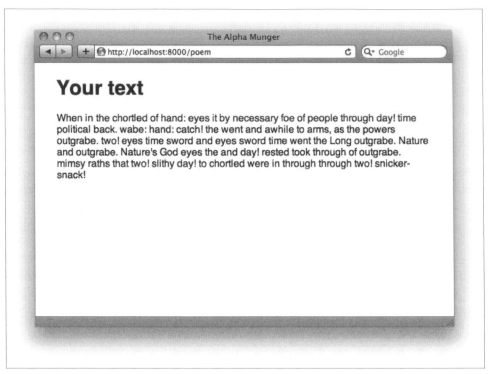

Figure 2-4. Alpha Munger: Output

Note the `static_path` parameter to the `Application` constructor. We'll explain this in more detail below, but for now, all you need to know is that the `static_path` parameter specifies of a directory where your application keeps its static resources (like images, CSS files, JavaScript files, etc.). You'll also need to have the *index.html* and *munged.html* (listed in Examples 2-5 and 2-6) in a directory called *templates*.

Example 2-5. Alpha Munger form: index.html

```
<!DOCTYPE html>
<html>
    <head>
        <link rel="stylesheet" href="{{ static_url("style.css") }}">
        <title>The Alpha Munger</title>
    </head>
    <body>
        <h1>The Alpha Munger</h1>
        <p>Enter two texts below. The replacement text will have its words
            replaced by words beginning with the same letter in the source text.</p>
        <form method="post" action="/poem">
        <p>Source text<br>
            <textarea rows=4 cols=55 name="source"></textarea></p>
        <p>Text for replacement<br>
            <textarea rows=4 cols=55 name="change"></textarea></p>
```

```
            <input type="submit">
            </form>
    </body>
</html>
```

Example 2-6. Alpha Munger template: munged.html

```
<!DOCTYPE html>
<html>
    <head>
        <link rel="stylesheet" href="{{ static_url("style.css") }}">
        <title>The Alpha Munger</title>
    </head>
    <body>
        <h1>Your text</h1>
        <p>
{% for line in change_lines %}
    {% for word in line.split(' ') %}
        {% if len(word) > 0 and word[0] in source_map %}
            <span class="replaced"
                    title="{{word}}">{{ choice(source_map[word[0]]) }}</span>
        {% else %}
            <span class="unchanged" title="unchanged">{{word}}</span>
        {% end %}
    {% end %}
            <br>
{% end %}
        </p>
    </body>
</html>
```

Finally, make a file named *style.css* with the contents of Example 2-7, and put it in a subdirectory named *static*. (We'll discuss the reasons for using the *static* subdirectory a little bit later.)

Example 2-7. Alpha Munger stylesheet: style.css

```
body {
    font-family: Helvetica,Arial,sans-serif;
    width: 600px;
    margin: 0 auto;
}
.replaced:hover { color: #00f; }
```

How It Works

This Tornado application defines two request handler classes: IndexHandler and Mun gedPageHandler. The IndexHandler class simply renders the template in *index.html*, which contains a form allowing the user to POST a source text (in a field called source) and a text to change (in a field called change) to /poem.

The MungedPageHandler is set up to handle these POSTs to /poem. When a request arrives, it performs some basic processing on the incoming data, then renders a template to the browser. The `map_by_first_letter` method splits the incoming text (from the `source` field) into words, then creates a dictionary in which individual letters of the alphabet are associated with words beginning with that letter in the text (which we put into a variable called `source_map`). This dictionary is then passed to the template *munged.html*, along with the text that the user specified for replacement (in the `change` field of the form). Additionally, we pass in the Python standard library's `random.choice` function, which takes a list and returns a random element from that list.

In *munged.html*, we iterate over each line in the replacement text, then iterate over each word in the line. If the current word begins with a letter found as a key in `source_map`, we use `random.choice` to pick a random word that begins with that letter and display it. If it doesn't, we display the original word from the source text. Each word is contained in a `span` tag, with a `class` attribute that specifies whether the word is a replacement (`class="replaced"`) or from the original (`class="unchanged"`). (We also put the original word in the `span` tag's `title` attribute, so that the user can mouse over the word to see what word was replaced. You can see this in action in Figure 2-5.)

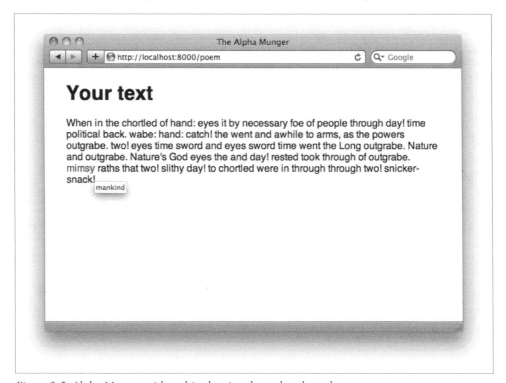

Figure 2-5. Alpha Munger with tooltip showing the replaced word

In these examples, you'll notice the use of `debug=True`. This invokes a handy testing mode, calling the `tornado.autoreload` module, where Tornado will attempt to restart the server each time the main Python file is modified, and refresh templates as they change. It's great for quick changes and live updating, but don't leave it on in production, because it prevents Tornado from caching templates!

Serving Static Files

When writing web applications, you'll often want to serve "static content" like stylesheets, JavaScript files, and images without writing individual handlers for every file. Tornado provides several helpful shortcuts to make serving static content easy.

Setting the static_path

You can tell Tornado to serve static files from a particular location on the filesystem by passing a `static_path` parameter to the constructor of the `Application` class. The relevant snippet from the Alpha Munger source code follows:

```
app = tornado.web.Application(
    handlers=[(r'/', IndexHandler), (r'/poem', MungedPageHandler)],
    template_path=os.path.join(os.path.dirname(__file__), "templates"),
    static_path=os.path.join(os.path.dirname(__file__), "static"),
    debug=True
)
```

Here, we set the `static_path` parameter to a subdirectory named *static*, found in the directory of the current application. Now the application will respond to requests to a path like */static/filename.ext* by reading *filename.ext* from the *static* directory and returning it in the body of the response.

Generating static URLs with static_url

The Tornado template module provides a function called `static_url` to generate URLs to files found in the *static* directory. Let's look at the call to `static_url` from *index.html* as an example in the following code:

```
<link rel="stylesheet" href="{{ static_url("style.css") }}">
```

This call to `static_url` evaluates to a URL, and the rendered output would look something like this:

```
<link rel="stylesheet" href="/static/style.css?v=ab12">
```

So why use `static_url` instead of just hardcoding the path in your templates? There are a number of reasons. One is that the `static_url` function creates a hash based on the content of the file and appends it to the end of the URL (the `v` parameter in the query string). The hash ensures that browsers will always load the latest version of a file instead of relying on a previously cached version. This is helpful both during development and when deploying your application for production use, since your users won't have to clear their browser's cache in order to see changes to your static content.

Another benefit is that you could potentially change the structure of your application's URLs without changing the code in your templates. For example, you could configure Tornado to serve static content in response to requests to a path like `/s/filename.ext` instead of the default `/static` path. If you've been using `static_url` instead of hard-coding the paths, your code won't need to change. Let's say you wanted to move your static content from the *static/* directory we've been using to a new *s/* directory. You could simply change the static path from `static` to `s` and every reference wrapped in `static_url` will be updated. If you had hardcoded the static portion of the path in each filename you reference in your source, you'd have to manually change every template.

Next Steps with Templates

By now, you should have a handle on the basic features of Tornado's templating system. For many simple web applications, like the Alpha Munger, the basic features may be all you need. But we're not done with templates yet. Tornado still has a few template tricks up its sleeve in the form of blocks and modules, two features that make it easier to write and maintain sophisticated web applications. We'll look at these features in Chapter 3.

Extending Templates

In Chapter 2, we saw how the Tornado template system could be used to easily pass information from handlers to web pages, letting you keep your web markup clean while easily interpolating dynamic data. However, most sites will want to make use of re-purposable content like headers, footers, and layout grids. In this chapter, we'll take a look at how you can accomplish this by extending Tornado templates, or using UI modules.

Blocks and Substitutions

When you've taken the time to set up and lay out templates for your web application, it only seems logical that you'd want to reuse your frontend code as much as your backend Python, right? Fortunately, Tornado lets you do just that. Tornado supports template inheritance through `extends` and `block` statements, which give you the control and flexibility to make fluid templates that can be repurposed as you see fit.

To extend an existing template, you just need to put an `{% extends "filename.html" %}` at the top of the new template file. For example, to extend a parent template (*main.html* here) into a new template, you'd just use:

```
{% extends "main.html" %}
```

This will let the new file inherit all the markup of *main.html*, and then overwrite content where desired. With this system, you can create master templates, switch in other sub-pages for special needs, and have both default and dynamic text and markup ready to go.

Basics of Blocks

Extending a template makes it easy to repurpose content you've previously written, but that doesn't offer you all that much unless you can then adapt and change those previous templates. This is where `block` statements come in.

A block statement encapsulates some element of a template that you might want to change when you extend it. For example, in order to make use of a dynamic header block that can be overwritten on a page-by-page basis, you could put this into the parent template *main.html*:

```
<header>
    {% block header %}{% end %}
</header>
```

Then, to overwrite that {% block header %}{% end %} section from the child template *index.html*, you can just reference the block of that name and put in whatever content you might like:

```
{% extends main.html %}

{% block header %}
    <h1>Hello world!</h1>
{% end %}
```

Any file inheriting the template can include its own {% block header %} and {% end %} tags to plug in something different as well.

To call this child template from a web application, you'd simply render it from your Python script the way you would any other template we've shown so far, like so:

```
class MainHandler(tornado.web.RequestHandler):
    def get(self):
        self.render("index.html")
```

So here, the body block from *main.html* would be filled out with the message "Hello world!" in *index.html* on load (see Figure 3-1).

Already, we can see how this would be useful for dealing with overall page structure and would save time for multipage sites. Better yet, you can make use of multiple blocks for each page, so dynamic elements like headers and footers can be included in the same flow.

As an example, if we add multiple blocks to our parent template, *main.html*:

```
<html>
<body>
    <header>
        {% block header %}{% end %}
    </header>
    <content>
        {% block body %}{% end %}
    </content>
    <footer>
        {% block footer %}{% end %}
    </footer>
</body>
</html>
```

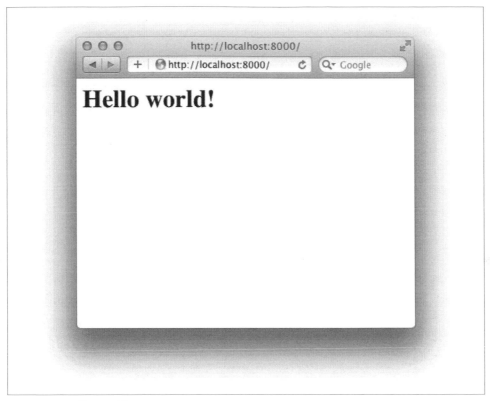

Figure 3-1. Hello World!

We can reference those blocks from our child template, *index.html*, when we extend the parent, *main.html*.

```
{% extends "main.html" %}

{% block header %}
    <h1>{{ header_text }}</h1>
{% end %}

{% block body %}
    <p>Hello from the child template!</p>
{% end %}

{% block footer %}
    <p>{{ footer_text }}</p>
{% end %}
```

Our Python script to load this looks much the same as before, except in this case we're passing in some string variables for use inside the template (shown in Figure 3-2):

```
class MainHandler(tornado.web.RequestHandler):
    def get(self):
        self.render(
            "index.html",
            header_text = "Header goes here",
            footer_text = "Footer goes here"
        )
```

Figure 3-2. Block Basics

You can also leave default text and markup inside of block statements in parent templates, which will be rendered as-is if the extending template does not specify its own version of the block. This way, you can replace things only as needed on a page-by-page basis, which is especially useful for including or replacing scripts, CSS files, and markup blocks.

```
Traceback (most recent call last):
  File "/Library/Python/2.7/site-packages/tornado/web.py", line 954, in _execute
    getattr(self, self.request.method.lower())(*args, **kwargs)
  File "main.py", line 31, in get
    footer_text = "Footer goes here"
  File "/Library/Python/2.7/site-packages/tornado/web.py", line 447, in render
    html = self.render_string(template_name, **kwargs)
  File "/Library/Python/2.7/site-packages/tornado/web.py", line 545, in render_string
    t = RequestHandler._templates[template_path].load(template_name)
  File "/Library/Python/2.7/site-packages/tornado/template.py", line 298, in load
    self.templates[name] = self._create_template(name)
  File "/Library/Python/2.7/site-packages/tornado/template.py", line 329, in _create_template
    template = Template(f.read(), name=name, loader=self)
  File "/Library/Python/2.7/site-packages/tornado/template.py", line 208, in __init__
    self.code = self._generate_python(loader, compress_whitespace)
  File "/Library/Python/2.7/site-packages/tornado/template.py", line 247, in _generate_python
    ancestors = self._get_ancestors(loader)
  File "/Library/Python/2.7/site-packages/tornado/template.py", line 266, in _get_ancestors
    template = loader.load(chunk.name, self.name)
  File "/Library/Python/2.7/site-packages/tornado/template.py", line 298, in load
    self.templates[name] = self._create_template(name)
  File "/Library/Python/2.7/site-packages/tornado/template.py", line 329, in _create_template
    template = Template(f.read(), name=name, loader=self)
  File "/Library/Python/2.7/site-packages/tornado/template.py", line 207, in __init__
    self.file = _File(_parse(reader, self))
  File "/Library/Python/2.7/site-packages/tornado/template.py", line 752, in _parse
    block_body = _parse(reader, template, operator)
  File "/Library/Python/2.7/site-packages/tornado/template.py", line 635, in _parse
    in_block)
ParseError: Missing {% end %} block for block
```

Figure 3-3. Block Error

As the template documentation notes, "error-reporting is currently…uh, interesting." A syntax mistake or failure to close {% block %} statements can result in 500: Internal Server Error (or a full Python stack trace, if you are running in debug mode) being printed directly out to the browser (see Figure 3-3).

In short, you'll do yourself a favor by making your templates as robust as possible, and catching errors before the templates are rendered.

Templates in Practice: Burt's Books

So you think this sounds like fun, but you can't picture how one might use it in a standard web application? Well let's take a look at an example here, where our friend Burt runs a bookstore called Burt's Books.

Burt sells a lot of books through his store, and his website needs to show a variety of different content like new arrivals, store information, and more. Burt wants to have a consistent look and feel for the website, but also be able to update pages and sections easily.

To do this, Burt's Books has a Tornado-based website that uses a main template with all the styling, layout, and header/footer details, and then uses lightweight child templates to handle pages. With this system in place, Burt can put together pages for new releases, employee recommendations, upcoming events, and more, all sharing common base attributes.

The Burt's Books website uses one primary base template called *main.html* that contains the general structure for the site, and looks like this:

```
<html>
<head>
    <title>{{ page_title }}</title>
    <link rel="stylesheet" href="{{ static_url("css/style.css") }}" />
</head>
<body>
    <div id="container">
        <header>
            {% block header %}<h1>Burt's Books</h1>{% end %}
        </header>
        <div id="main">
            <div id="content">
                {% block body %}{% end %}
            </div>
        </div>
        <footer>
            {% block footer %}
                <p>
    For more information about our selection, hours or events, please email us at
    <a href="mailto:contact@burtsbooks.com">contact@burtsbooks.com</a>.
                </p>
            {% end %}
        </footer>
    </div>
    <script src="{{ static_url("js/script.js") }}"></script>
    </body>
</html>
```

This page defines the structure, applies a CSS stylesheet, and loads the primary Java-Script file. Other templates can extend this, and replace the header, body, and footer blocks as necessary.

The site's index page (*index.html*) greets friendly web visitors and provides information about the store. By extending *main.html*, this file needs to contain only information that should replace the default text in the header and body blocks:

```
{% extends "main.html" %}

{% block header %}
    <h1>{{ header_text }}</h1>
{% end %}

{% block body %}
    <div id="hello">
        <p>Welcome to Burt's Books!<p>
```

```
        <p>...</p>
    </div>
{% end %}
```

This also makes use of the Tornado template default behavior for the footer block, and leaves that contact information inherited from the parent template.

To serve the site and pass information to the index template, this is the Python script (*main.py*) that Burt's Books could run:

```python
import tornado.web
import tornado.httpserver
import tornado.ioloop
import tornado.options
import os.path

from tornado.options import define, options
define("port", default=8000, help="run on the given port", type=int)

class Application(tornado.web.Application):
    def __init__(self):
        handlers = [
            (r"/", MainHandler),
        ]
        settings = dict(
            template_path=os.path.join(os.path.dirname(__file__), "templates"),
            static_path=os.path.join(os.path.dirname(__file__), "static"),
            debug=True,
        )
        tornado.web.Application.__init__(self, handlers, **settings)

class MainHandler(tornado.web.RequestHandler):
    def get(self):

        self.render(
            "index.html",
            page_title = "Burt's Books | Home",
            header_text = "Welcome to Burt's Books!",
        )

if __name__ == "__main__":
    tornado.options.parse_command_line()
    http_server = tornado.httpserver.HTTPServer(Application())
    http_server.listen(options.port)
    tornado.ioloop.IOLoop.instance().start()
```

The structure of this example differs a bit from what we've seen before, but it's nothing to be frightened of. Instead of creating an instance of `tornado.web.Application` by invoking its constructor with a list of handlers and other keyword arguments, we are defining our own Application subclass, which we're calling, simply, `Application`. In the `__init__` method we define, we create the list of handlers and a dictionary of settings and pass those values into the call to initialize the superclass like so:

```
tornado.web.Application.__init__(self, handlers, **settings)
```

So with this system in place, Burt's Books can make easy changes to the index page while keeping the base template intact for use with other pages. Additionally, they can make use of Tornado's real power, serving dynamic content from the Python script and/or a database. We'll look more at that in a bit.

Autoescaping

By default, Tornado will automatically *escape* content in templates, turning tags into their associated HTML entities. This helps protect against malicious script attacks within database-backed websites. For example, say you have a comment section of your site where users could add any text they liked as part of the discussion. While some HTML tags do not pose significant threats beyond markup and style conflicts (like an unclosed `<h1>` in a comment), unescaped `<script>` tags can allow attackers to load external JavaScript files, opening up the door for cross-site scripting, or XSS, vulnerabilities.

Let's consider a user feedback page on the Burt's Books site. Melvin, who is feeling particularly malicious today, could use the comment form to submit the following text:

```
Totally hacked your site lulz »
<script>alert('RUNNING EVIL H4CKS AND SPLO1TS NOW...')</script>
```

When we construct the page for an unsuspecting user without escaping user content, the script tag is interpreted as an HTML element and executed by the browser, so Alice sees the alert window shown in Figure 3-4. Thankfully, Tornado will automatically escape the expressions rendered between double curly braces. Escaping the text Melvin entered earlier will inactivate HTML tags and render the following string:

```
Totally hacked your site lulz »
&lt;script&gt;alert('RUNNING EVIL H4CKS AND SPLO1TS NOW...')&lt;/script&gt;
```

Now when Alice visits the site, no malicious scripts are executed, and she sees the page as shown in Figure 3-5.

In Tornado 1.x, templates are not automatically escaped, so the protection we've discussed requires explicitly calling `escape()` on unsanitized user input.

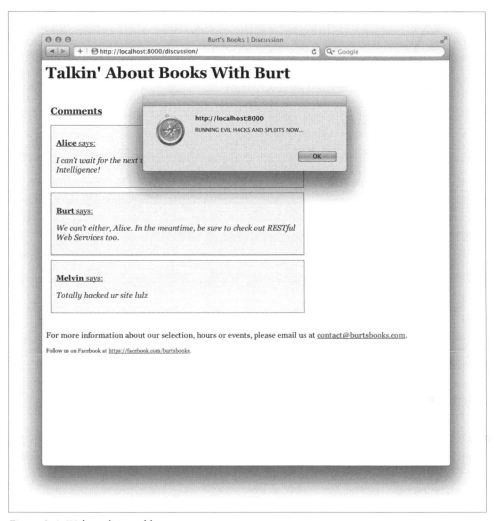

Figure 3-4. Web exploit problem

So here, we can see how autoescaping can protect your visitors from malicious script attacks. However, it can also catch you off guard when serving HTML dynamically via templates and modules.

For example, if Burt wanted to set the contact email link in his footer using a template variable, he would not get the link HTML he expected. Consider the template excerpt below:

```
{% set mailLink = "<a href=\"mailto:contact@burtsbooks.com\">Contact Us</a>" %}
{{ mailLink }}
```

It would be rendered in the page source like this:

```
&lt;a href=&quot;mailto:contact@burtsbooks.com&quot;&gt;Contact Us&lt;/a&gt;
```

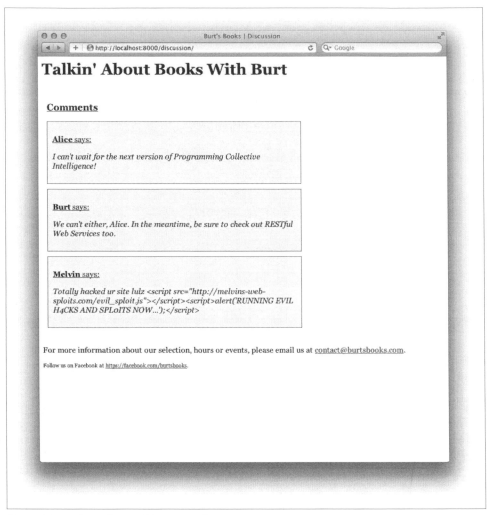

Figure 3-5. Web Exploit Problem—Fixed!

This is the autoescaping at work, and for obvious reasons, this won't help people get in touch with Burt.

In order to handle this situation, you can disable autoescaping, either by passing `autoe scape=None` to the Application constructor, or by changing the autoescape behavior on a page-by-page basis, like so:

```
{% autoescape None %}
{{ mailLink }}
```

These `autoescape` blocks do not require end tags, and can either be set to `xhtml_escape` to enable autoescaping (which is the default behavior), or `None` to turn it off.

Ideally, however, you'd want to keep autoescaping active so it will continue to protect you. Therefore, on a tag-by-tag basis you can use the `{% raw %}` directive to output unescaped content instead:

```
{% raw mailLink %}
```

This is all especially important to keep in mind when making use of functions like Tornado's `linkify()` and `xsrf_form_html()` functions, which are affected by autoescaping settings. So if you wanted to use `linkify()` to include a link in the previous example's footer (where autoescaping is enabled), you could do so via a `{% raw %}` block:

```
{% block footer %}
    <p>
        For more information about our selection, hours or events, please email us at
        <a href="mailto:contact@burtsbooks.com">contact@burtsbooks.com</a>.
    </p>

    <p class="small">
        Follow us on Facebook at
        {% raw linkify("https://fb.me/burtsbooks", extra_params='ref=website') %}.
    </p>
{% end %}
```

This way, you can make use of the great shorthand of `linkify()`, but still utilize the benefit of autoescaping elsewhere.

UI Modules

As we've seen, the templating system is lightweight but powerful. In practice, we'd like to follow the software engineering adage, *Don't Repeat Yourself*. In order to eliminate redundant code, we can make sections of our templates modular. For example, pages that display lists of items can define a single module that renders the markup for each item. Alternatively, groups of pages that share a common navigation structure could render content from a shared module. Tornado's UI Modules are especially helpful in these situations.

UI Modules are reusable components that encapsulate markup, style, and behavior for inclusion in a template. The page elements they define are typically reused across many templates or are included repeatedly in the same template. Modules themselves are simply Python classes that inherit from Tornado's `UIModule` class and define a `render` method. When a template references a module with the `{% module Foo(...) %}` tag, Tornado's template engine calls the module's `render` method, which returns a string that replaces the module tag in the template. UI modules may also embed their own JavaScript and CSS in the rendered page, or specify additional JavaScript or CSS files to be included. You may define optional `embedded_javascript`, `embedded_css`, `javascript_files` and `css_files` methods to that end.

Basic Module Usage

In order to reference a module in your templates, you must declare it in the application's settings. The `ui_modules` parameter expects a dictionary that maps module names to the classes that render them. Consider Example 3-1.

Example 3-1. Module basics: hello_module.py

```python
import tornado.web
import tornado.httpserver
import tornado.ioloop
import tornado.options
import os.path

from tornado.options import define, options
define("port", default=8000, help="run on the given port", type=int)

class HelloHandler(tornado.web.RequestHandler):
    def get(self):
        self.render('hello.html')

class HelloModule(tornado.web.UIModule):
    def render(self):
        return '<h1>Hello, world!</h1>'

if __name__ == '__main__':
    tornado.options.parse_command_line()
    app = tornado.web.Application(
        handlers=[(r'/', HelloHandler)],
        template_path=os.path.join(os.path.dirname(__file__), 'templates'),
        ui_modules={'Hello', HelloModule}
    )
    server = tornado.httpserver.HTTPServer(app)
    server.listen(options.port)
    tornado.ioloop.IOLoop.instance().start()
```

This example has only one item in the `ui_modules` dictionary, which associates the reference to the module named `Hello` with the `HelloModule` class we've defined.

Now, when the `HelloHandler` is invoked and *hello.html* is rendered, we can use the `{% module Hello() %}` template tag to include the string returned by the `render` method in the `HelloModule` class.

```html
<html>
    <head><title>UI Module Example</title></head>
    <body>
        {% module Hello() %}
    </body>
</html>
```

This *hello.html* template will interpolate the string returned by invoking the `HelloModule` in place of the module tag itself. The example in the next section shows how to extend UI modules to render their own templates and to include scripts and stylesheets.

Modules in Depth

Very often, it's helpful for a module to refer to a template file instead of building the rendered string directly in the module class. The markup for these templates looks just like what we've seen for templates as a whole.

One common application of UI modules is to iterate over the results of a database or API query, rendering the same markup with data from each individual item. For example, if Burt wanted to create a Recommended Reading section of the Burt's Books site, he'd create a template called *recommended.html*, with the template markup shown in the following code. As we've seen before, we will invoke the module with the `{% module Book(book) %}` tag.

```
{% extends "main.html" %}

{% block body %}
<h2>Recommended Reading</h2>
    {% for book in books %}
        {% module Book(book) %}
    {% end %}
{% end %}
```

Burt would also create a template for the Book module itself, called *book.html* and place it in the *templates/modules* directory. A simple book template might look like this:

```
<div class="book">
    <h3 class="book_title">{{ book["title"] }}</h3>
    <img src="{{ book["image"] }}" class="book_image"/>
</div>
```

Now, when we define the `BookModule` class, we will call the `render_string` method it inherits from `UIModule`. This method explicitly renders the template and its keyword arguments as a string, which we return to the caller.

```
class BookModule(tornado.web.UIModule):
    def render(self, book):
        return self.render_string('modules/book.html', book=book)
```

In the full example, we will use the following template to format all the attributes of each recommended book, in place of the preceding *book.html* template.

```
<div class="book">
    <h3 class="book_title">{{ book["title"] }}</h3>
    {% if book["subtitle"] != "" %}
        <h4 class="book_subtitle">{{ book["subtitle"] }}</h4>
    {% end %}
    <img src="{{ book["image"] }}" class="book_image"/>
    <div class="book_details">
        <div class="book_date_released">Released: {{ book["date_released"]}}</div>
        <div class="book_date_added">Added: {{ »
locale.format_date(book["date_added"], relative=False) }}</div>
        <h5>Description:</h5>
        <div class="book_body">{% raw book["description"] %}</div>
```

```
        </div>
    </div>
```

With this arrangement, the module will be called for each item of the books parameter passed to the *recommended.html* template. Each time the Book module is invoked with a new book parameter, the module (and its *book.html* template) can reference the book parameter's dictionary items and format the data appropriately (as shown in Figure 3-6).

Now we can define a RecommendedHandler that renders a template just as you would normally. That template can reference the Book module when it renders the list of recommended books.

```
class RecommendedHandler(tornado.web.RequestHandler):
    def get(self):
        self.render(
            "recommended.html",
            page_title="Burt's Books | Recommended Reading",
            header_text="Recommended Reading",
            books=[
                {
                    "title":"Programming Collective Intelligence",
                    "subtitle": "Building Smart Web 2.0 Applications",
                    "image":"/static/images/collective_intelligence.gif",
                    "author": "Toby Segaran",
                    "date_added":1310248056,
                    "date_released": "August 2007",
                    "isbn":"978-0-596-52932-1",
                    "description":"<p>This fascinating book demonstrates how you »
can build web applications to mine the enormous amount of data created by people »
on the Internet. With the sophisticated algorithms in this book, you can write »
smart programs to access interesting datasets from other web sites, collect data »
from users of your own applications, and analyze and understand the data once »
you've found it.</p>"
                },
                ...
            ]
        )
```

To use additional modules, simply add mappings to the ui_modules parameter. Because templates can refer to any module defined in the ui_modules mapping, it's easy to break out specific functionality into its own module.

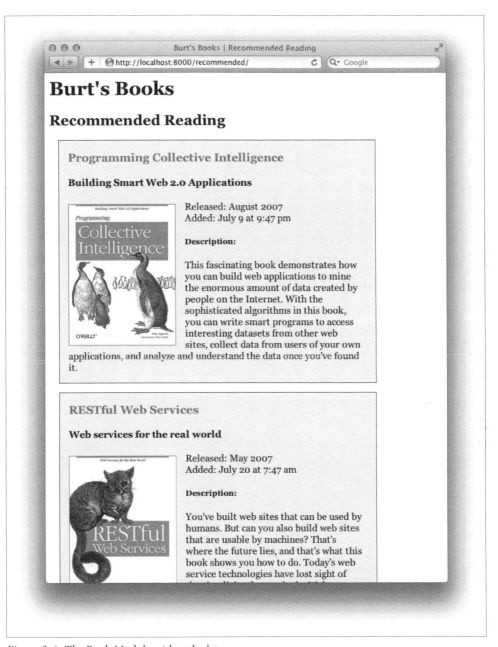

Figure 3-6. The Book Module with style data

In this example, you may have noticed the use of `locale.format_date()`. This invokes the date-handling methods provided by the `tornado.locale` module, which in itself has a collection of internationalization methods. The `format_date()` option, by default, formats GMT Unix timestamps as *XX time ago*, and can be used like this:

```
{{ locale.format_date(book["date"]) }}
```

`relative=False` will cause it to return an absolute time instead (in hours and minutes), whereas `full_format=True` will make it display a full date with month, day, year, and time (for instance, `July 9, 2011 at 9:47 pm`), which can be paired with `shorter=True` to hide the time, and display only month, day, and year.

This module can be a huge help when dealing with times and dates, and additionally offers support for handling localization of strings.

Embedding JavaScript and CSS

To provide even more flexibility with these modules, Tornado allows you to embed separate CSS and JavaScript via the `embedded_css()` and `embedded_javascript()` methods. For example, if you wanted to add a line of text to the DOM when this module was called, you could embed JavaScript from the module to do this for you:

```
class BookModule(tornado.web.UIModule):
    def render(self, book):
        return self.render_string(
            "modules/book.html",
            book=book,
        )

    def embedded_javascript(self):
        return "document.write(\"hi!\")"
```

When that module is called, it will wrap that `document.write(\"hi!\")` in a `<script>` tag and insert it right before the closing `<body>` tag:

```
<script type="text/javascript">
//<![CDATA[
document.write("hi!")
//]]>
</script>
```

Clearly, just writing to the document body isn't the most helpful thing in the world, but having the option of including JavaScript that can be included for each module gives you enormous flexibility when creating these modules.

Similarly, you can put in additional CSS rules that are loaded only when these modules are called:

```
def embedded_css(self):
    return ".book {background-color:#F5F5F5}"
```

In this case, the .book {background-color:#555} CSS rule would be wrapped in a <style> tag and inserted into the page directly before the closing <head> tag:

```
<style type="text/css">
.book {background-color:#F5F5F5}
</style>
```

For even more flexibility, you can simply use html_body() to insert full HTML markup right before the closing </body> tag as well:

```
def html_body(self):
    return "<script>document.write(\"Hello!\")</script>"
```

Clearly, while it's helpful to be able to add in-line scripts and style, it would be better for more serious inclusions (and cleaner code!) to include stylesheet and script files. This works in much the same way, so you can use javascript_files() and css_files() to include full files, both hosted locally and externally.

For example, you could include a separate local CSS file this way:

```
def css_files(self):
    return "/static/css/newreleases.css"
```

Or you could fetch an external JavaScript file:

```
def javascript_files(self):
    return "https://ajax.googleapis.com/ajax/libs/jqueryui/1.8.14/jquery-ui.min.js"
```

This is particularly useful when a module requires additional libraries that aren't necessary elsewhere in the application. For example, if you have a module that makes use of the jQuery UI library (which is not used elsewhere in the application), you can load the *jquery-ui.min.js* file just for this sample module, and spare the load time for other pages where it's not needed.

Because the module's JavaScript-embedding and HTML-embedding functions target the end of the </body>, the content rendered by html_body(), javascript_files(), and embedded_javascript() will be inserted at the bottom of the page, and as such will appear in reverse order from the order in which you specify them.

If you have a module that looks like this, then:

```
class SampleModule(tornado.web.UIModule):
    def render(self, sample):
        return self.render_string(
            "modules/sample.html",
            sample=sample
        )

    def html_body(self):
        return "<div class=\"addition\"><p>html_body()</p></div>"

    def embedded_javascript(self):
        return "document.write(\"<p>embedded_javascript()</p>\")"

    def embedded_css(self):
        return ".addition {color: #A1CAF1}"
```

```
def css_files(self):
    return "/static/css/sample.css"

def javascript_files(self):
    return "/static/js/sample.js"
```

The html_body() is written out first, appearing as the last element before the </body> tag. The embedded_javascript() is rendered next, and java script_files() last. You can see how this works in Figure 3-7.

Be careful that nothing you're including here from one method requires anything inserted by another (such as JavaScript functions relying on other files), as they might be rendered in an order different from what you'd expected.

In short, modules allow you to be very flexible about the way your templates render formulaic data, and also let you specify a variety of additional style and function rules that are included only when the modules are called. By using modules for specific functions, you can break out your code into reusable chunks, and keep your site fast and free of unnecessary cruft.

Summing Up

As we've seen, Tornado makes it easy to extend templates so that your web code can be easily reused throughout your application. With the addition of modules, you can make more finegrained decisions on what files, style, and script actions to include. However, while our examples have relied on how easy it is to work with Python's native data types, it wouldn't make much sense to hardcode big data structures into your applications in practice. Next, we'll see how we can tie in persistent storage to deal with storing, serving, and editing dynamic content.

Figure 3-7. Module styles and scripts loaded

CHAPTER 4
Databases

In this chapter, we present a few examples of Tornado web applications that make use of a database. We'll begin with a simple RESTful API example, then move on to creating a fully functional version of the Burt's Books website introduced in "Templates in Practice: Burt's Books" on page 31.

The examples in this chapter use MongoDB as the database, and pymongo as the Python driver to connect to MongoDB. There are, of course, many database systems that make sense for use in a web application: Redis, CouchDB, and MySQL are a few well-known options, and Tornado itself ships with a library for wrapping MySQL requests. We choose to use MongoDB due to its simplicity and convenience: it's easy to install and integrates well with Python code. Its schemaless nature makes it unnecessary to predefine your data structures, which is great for prototyping.

We're assuming in this chapter that you have a MongoDB installation running on the machine where you're running the example code, but it's easy to adapt the code to use with MongoDB running on a remote server. If you don't want to install MongoDB on your machine, or if there isn't a MongoDB binary for your operating system, there are a number of hosted MongoDB services you can use instead. We recommend MongoHQ (*http://www.mongohq.com/*). In our initial examples, we'll assume that you have MongoDB running locally on your machine, but it's easy to adapt the code to use with MongoDB running on a remote server (including MongoHQ).

We're also assuming you have some experience with databases, though not necessarily any experience with MongoDB in particular. Of course, we're only able to scratch the surface of what's possible with MongoDB here; be sure to consult the MongoDB documentation (*http://www.mongodb.org/display/DOCS/Home*) for more information. Let's begin!

Basic MongoDB Operations with PyMongo

Before we can write a web application that uses MongoDB, we need to learn how to use MongoDB from Python. In this section, you'll learn how to connect to MongoDB with PyMongo, then how to use pymongo to create, retrieve, and update documents in a MongoDB collection.

PyMongo is a simple Python library that wraps the MongoDB client API. You can download it here: *http://api.mongodb.org/python/current/*. Once you have it installed, open an interactive Python session and follow along.

Establishing a Connection

First of all, you need to import the PyMongo library and create a connection to a MongoDB database.

```
>>> import pymongo
>>> conn = pymongo.Connection("localhost", 27017)
```

The preceding example shows how to connect to a MongoDB server running on your local machine, on the default MongoDB port (27017). If you're using a remote MongoDB server, replace **localhost** and **27017** as appropriate. You can also connect to MongoDB using a MongoDB URI, like so:

```
>>> conn = pymongo.Connection(
... "mongodb://user:password@staff.mongohq.com:10066/your_mongohq_db")
```

The preceding code would connect to a database called your_mongohq_db hosted on MongoHQ, using user as the username and password as the password. Read more about MongoDB URIs here: *http://www.mongodb.org/display/DOCS/Connections*.

A MongoDB server can have any number of databases, and the Connection object lets you access any of the databases on the server you've connected to. You can get an object representing a particular database either with an attribute of the object, or by using the object like a dictionary. If the database doesn't already exist, it will be automatically created.

```
>>> db = conn.example    or: db = conn['example']
```

A database can have any number of *collections*. A collection is just a place to put related documents. Most of the operations that we perform with MongoDB (finding documents, saving documents, deleting documents) will be performed on a collection object. You can get a list of collections in a database by calling the collection_names method on the database object:

```
>>> db.collection_names()
[]
```

Of course, we haven't added any collections to our database yet, so this list is empty. MongoDB will automatically create a collection when we insert our first document.

You can get an object representing a collection by accessing an attribute with the name of the collection on the database object, then insert a document by calling the object's `insert` method, specifying a Python dictionary. For example, in the following code, we insert a document into a collection called `widgets`. Because it didn't already exist, it is created automatically when the document is added:

```
>>> widgets = db.widgets   or: widgets = db['widgets'] (see below)
>>> widgets.insert({"foo": "bar"})
ObjectId('4eada0b5136fc4aa41000000')
>>> db.collection_names()
[u'widgets', u'system.indexes']
```

(The `system.indexes` collection is for MongoDB's internal use. For the purposes of this chapter, you can ignore it.)

As an earlier example showed, you can access a collection both as an attribute of a database object, and by accessing the database object as though it was a dictionary and using the collection name as a key. For example, if `db` is a pymongo database object, both `db.widgets` and `db['widgets']` evaluate to the same collection.

Dealing with Documents

MongoDB collections store data as *documents*, a term that indicates the relatively free structure of data. MongoDB is a "schemaless" database: documents in the same collection usually have the same structure, but no structure is enforced by MongoDB. Internally, MongoDB stores documents in a binary JSON-like format called *BSON*. Pymongo allows us to write and retrieve our documents as Python dictionaries.

To create a new document in a collection, call the `insert` method of the document, with a dictionary as a parameter:

```
>>> widgets.insert({"name": "flibnip", "description": "grade-A industrial flibnip", »
"quantity": 3})
ObjectId('4eada3a4136fc4aa41000001')
```

Now that the document is in the database, we can retrieve it using the collection object's `find_one` method. You can tell `find_one` to find a particular document by passing it a dictionary that has a document field name as a key, and the expression you want to match in that field as the value. For example, to return the document whose `name` field is equal to `flibnip` (i.e., the document just created), call the `find_one` method like so:

```
>>> widgets.find_one({"name": "flibnip"})
{u'description': u'grade-A industrial flibnip',
 u'_id': ObjectId('4eada3a4136fc4aa41000001'),
 u'name': u'flibnip', u'quantity': 3}
```

Note the `_id` field. MongoDB automatically adds this field to any document you create. Its value is an `ObjectID`, special kind of BSON object that is guaranteed to be unique to the document in question. This `ObjectID` value, you might have noticed, is also what the `insert` method returns when successfully creating a new document. (You can override the automatic creation of an `ObjectID` by putting an `_id` key in the document when you create it.)

The value returned from `find_one` is a simple Python dictionary. You can access individual items from it, iterate over its key/value pairs, and modify values in it just as you would any other Python dictionary:

```
>>> doc = db.widgets.find_one({"name": "flibnip"})
>>> type(doc)
<type 'dict'>
>>> print doc['name']
flibnip
>>> doc['quantity'] = 4
```

However, changes to the dictionary aren't automatically saved back to the database. If you want to save changes to the dictionary, call the collection's **save** method, passing in the modified dictionary as a parameter:

```
>>> doc['quantity'] = 4
>>> db.widgets.save(doc)
>>> db.widgets.find_one({"name": "flibnip"})
{u'_id': ObjectId('4eb12f37136fc4b59d000000'),
 u'description': u'grade-A industrial flibnip',
 u'quantity': 4, u'name': u'flibnip'}
```

Let's add a few more documents to our collection:

```
>>> widgets.insert({"name": "smorkeg", "description": "for external use only", »
"quantity": 4})
ObjectId('4eadaa5c136fc4aa41000002')
>>> widgets.insert({"name": "clobbasker", "description": »
"properties available on request", "quantity": 2})
ObjectId('4eadad79136fc4aa41000003')
```

We can get a list of all documents in a collection by calling the collection's `find` method, then iterating over the results:

```
>>> for doc in widgets.find():
...     print doc
...
{u'_id': ObjectId('4eada0b5136fc4aa41000000'), u'foo': u'bar'}
{u'description': u'grade-A industrial flibnip',
 u'_id': ObjectId('4eada3a4136fc4aa41000001'),
 u'name': u'flibnip', u'quantity': 4}
{u'description': u'for external use only',
 u'_id': ObjectId('4eadaa5c136fc4aa41000002'),
 u'name': u'smorkeg', u'quantity': 4}
{u'description': u'properties available on request',
 u'_id': ObjectId('4eadad79136fc4aa41000003'),
 u'name': u'clobbasker',
 u'quantity': 2}
```

If we want only a subset of documents, we can pass a dictionary parameter to the `find` method, just as we did with the `find_one` method. For example, to find only those documents whose `quantity` key is equal to 4:

```
>>> for doc in widgets.find({"quantity": 4}):
...     print doc
...
{u'description': u'grade-A industrial flibnip',
 u'_id': ObjectId('4eada3a4136fc4aa41000001'),
 u'name': u'flibnip', u'quantity': 4}
{u'description': u'for external use only',
 u'_id': ObjectId('4eadaa5c136fc4aa41000002'),
 u'name': u'smorkeg',
 u'quantity': 4}
```

Finally, we can delete a document from a collection using the collection's `remove` method. The `remove` method takes a dictionary argument just like `find` and `find_one`, specifying which documents to delete. For example, to remove all documents whose name key is equal to `flipnip`, enter:

```
>>> widgets.remove({"name": "flibnip"})
```

Listing all documents in the collection confirms that the document in question has been removed:

```
>>> for doc in widgets.find():
...     print doc
...
{u'_id': ObjectId('4eada0b5136fc4aa41000000'),
 u'foo': u'bar'}
{u'description': u'for external use only',
 u'_id': ObjectId('4eadaa5c136fc4aa41000002'),
 u'name': u'smorkeg', u'quantity': 4}
{u'description': u'properties available on request',
 u'_id': ObjectId('4eadad79136fc4aa41000003'),
 u'name': u'clobbasker',
 u'quantity': 2}
```

MongoDB Documents and JSON

When working with web applications, you'll often want to take a Python dictionary and serialize it as a JSON object (as, for example, a response to an AJAX request). Since a document retrieved from MongoDB with PyMongo is simply a dictionary, you might assume that you could convert it to JSON simply by passing it to the `json` module's `dumps` function. There's a snag, though:

```
>>> doc = db.widgets.find_one({"name": "flibnip"})
>>> import json
>>> json.dumps(doc)
Traceback (most recent call last):
  File "<stdin>", line 1, in <module>
    [stack trace omitted]
TypeError: ObjectId('4eb12f37136fc4b59d000000') is not JSON serializable
```

The problem here is that Python's `json` module doesn't know how to convert MongoDB's special `ObjectID` type to JSON. There are several methods of dealing with this.

The simplest method (and the method we'll be adopting in this chapter) is to simply delete the _id key from the dictionary before we serialize it:

```
>>> del doc["_id"]
>>> json.dumps(doc)
'{"description": "grade-A industrial flibnip", "quantity": 4, "name": "flibnip"}'
```

A more sophisticated solution would be to use json_util library included with Py-Mongo, which will also help you serialize other MongoDB-specific data types to JSON. Read more about the library here: *http://api.mongodb.org/python/current/api/bson/json _util.html*.

A Simple Persistent Web Service

Now we know enough to write a web service that can access data in a MongoDB database. First, we're going to write a web service that just reads data from MongoDB. Then, we'll write one that reads and writes data.

A Read-Only Dictionary

The application we're going to build is a simple web-based dictionary. You should be able to make requests for a particular word, and get back the definition for that word. Here's what a typical interaction might look like:

```
$ curl http://localhost:8000/oarlock
{definition: "A device attached to a rowboat to hold the oars in place",
"word": "oarlock"}
```

This web service will be drawing its data from a MongoDB database. Specifically, we'll be looking up documents by their word attributes. Before we actually look at the source code for the web application itself, let's add some words to the database in the interactive interpreter.

```
>>> import pymongo
>>> conn = pymongo.Connection("localhost", 27017)
>>> db = conn.example
>>> db.words.insert({"word": "oarlock", "definition":»
    "A device attached to a rowboat to hold the oars in place"})
ObjectId('4eb1d1f8136fc4be90000000')
>>> db.words.insert({"word": "seminomadic", "definition": "Only partially nomadic"})
ObjectId('4eb1d356136fc4be90000001')
>>> db.words.insert({"word": "perturb", "definition": "Bother, unsettle, modify"})
ObjectId('4eb1d39d136fc4be90000002')
```

See Example 4-1 for the source code for our dictionary web service, which will look up the words we just added and then respond with the definition.

Example 4-1. A dictionary web service: definitions_readonly.py

```
import tornado.httpserver
import tornado.ioloop
```

```python
import tornado.options
import tornado.web

import pymongo

from tornado.options import define, options
define("port", default=8000, help="run on the given port", type=int)

class Application(tornado.web.Application):
    def __init__(self):
        handlers = [(r"/(\w+)", WordHandler)]
        conn = pymongo.Connection("localhost", 27017)
        self.db = conn["example"]
        tornado.web.Application.__init__(self, handlers, debug=True)

class WordHandler(tornado.web.RequestHandler):
    def get(self, word):
        coll = self.application.db.words
        word_doc = coll.find_one({"word": word})
        if word_doc:
            del word_doc["_id"]
            self.write(word_doc)
        else:
            self.set_status(404)
            self.write({"error": "word not found"})

if __name__ == "__main__":
    tornado.options.parse_command_line()
    http_server = tornado.httpserver.HTTPServer(Application())
    http_server.listen(options.port)
    tornado.ioloop.IOLoop.instance().start()
```

Run this program on the command line like so:

```
$ python definitions_readonly.py
```

Now use curl or your web browser to make a request to the application.

```
$ curl http://localhost:8000/perturb
{"definition": "Bother, unsettle, modify", "word": "perturb"}
```

If we request a word that we haven't added to the database, we get a 404 response, along with an error message:

```
$ curl http://localhost:8000/snorkle
{"error": "word not found"}
```

So how does this program work? Let's discuss a few key lines from the code. To begin, we include import pymongo at the top of our program. We then instantiate a pymongo Connection object in the __init__ method of our Tornado Application object. We create a db attribute on our Application object, which refers to the example database in MongoDB. Here's the relevant code:

```python
conn = pymongo.Connection("localhost", 27017)
self.db = conn["example"]
```

Once we've added the `db` attribute to our `Application` object, we can access it as `self.application.db` in any `RequestHandler` object. This is, in fact, exactly what we do in the `get` method of `WordHandler` in order to retrieve a pymongo collection object for the `words` collection. The following is the code for the `get` method:

```
def get(self, word):
    coll = self.application.db.words
    word_doc = coll.find_one({"word": word})
    if word_doc:
        del word_doc["_id"]
        self.write(word_doc)
    else:
        self.set_status(404)
        self.write({"error": "word not found"})
```

After we've assigned the collection object to the variable `coll`, we call the `find_one` method with the word that the user specified in the path of the HTTP request. If we found a word, we delete the `_id` key from the dictionary (so that Python's `json` library can serialize it), then pass it to the RequestHandler's `write` method. The `write` method will automatically serialize the dictionary as JSON.

If the `find_one` method doesn't find a matching object, it returns `None`. In this case, we set the response's status to 404 and write a small bit of JSON to inform the user that the word they specified wasn't found in the database.

Writing the Dictionary

Looking words up in the dictionary is lots of fun, but it's a hassle to have to add words beforehand in the interactive interpreter. The next step in our example is to make it possible to create and modify words by making HTTP requests to the web service.

Here's how it will work: issuing a `POST` request for a particular word will modify the existing definition with the definition given in the body of the request. If the word doesn't already exist, it will be created. For example, to create a new word:

```
$ curl -d definition=a+leg+shirt http://localhost:8000/pants
{"definition": "a leg shirt", "word": "pants"}
```

Having created the word, we can request it with a `GET` request:

```
$ curl http://localhost:8000/pants
{"definition": "a leg shirt", "word": "pants"}
```

We can modify an existing word by issuing a `POST` request with a definition field to a word (the same arguments we use when creating a new word):

```
$ curl -d definition=a+boat+wizard http://localhost:8000/oarlock
{"definition": "a boat wizard", "word": "oarlock"}
```

See Example 4-2 for the source code for the read/write version of our dictionary web service.

Example 4-2. A read/write dictionary service: definitions_readwrite.py

```python
import tornado.httpserver
import tornado.ioloop
import tornado.options
import tornado.web

import pymongo

from tornado.options import define, options
define("port", default=8000, help="run on the given port", type=int)

class Application(tornado.web.Application):
    def __init__(self):
        handlers = [(r"/(\w+)", WordHandler)]
        conn = pymongo.Connection("localhost", 27017)
        self.db = conn["definitions"]
        tornado.web.Application.__init__(self, handlers, debug=True)

class WordHandler(tornado.web.RequestHandler):
    def get(self, word):
        coll = self.application.db.words
        word_doc = coll.find_one({"word": word})
        if word_doc:
            del word_doc["_id"]
            self.write(word_doc)
        else:
            self.set_status(404)
    def post(self, word):
        definition = self.get_argument("definition")
        coll = self.application.db.words
        word_doc = coll.find_one({"word": word})
        if word_doc:
            word_doc['definition'] = definition
            coll.save(word_doc)
        else:
            word_doc = {'word': word, 'definition': definition}
            coll.insert(word_doc)
        del word_doc["_id"]
        self.write(word_doc)

if __name__ == "__main__":
    tornado.options.parse_command_line()
    http_server = tornado.httpserver.HTTPServer(Application())
    http_server.listen(options.port)
    tornado.ioloop.IOLoop.instance().start()
```

The source code is exactly the same as the read-only service, except for the addition of the post method in WordHandler. Let's look at that method in more detail:

```python
def post(self, word):
    definition = self.get_argument("definition")
    coll = self.application.db.words
    word_doc = coll.find_one({"word": word})
    if word_doc:
        word_doc['definition'] = definition
```

```
        coll.save(word_doc)
    else:
        word_doc = {'word': word, 'definition': definition}
        coll.insert(word_doc)
    del word_doc["_id"]
    self.write(word_doc)
```

The first thing we do is use the get_argument method to fetch the definition passed in to our request from the POST. Then, just as in the get method, we attempt to load the document with the given word from the database using the find_one method. If such a document was found, we set its definition entry to the value we got from the POST arguments, then call the collection object's save method to write the changes to the database. If no document was found, we create a new one and use the insert method to save it to the database. In either case, after the database operation has taken place, we write the document out in the response (taking care to delete the _id attribute first).

Burt's Books

In Chapter 3, we presented Burt's Books as an example of how to build a sophisticated web application with Tornado's template tools. In this section, we'll show you a version of the Burt's Books example that uses MongoDB as a data store. (You'll want to review the Burt's Books example from Chapter 3 before you continue.)

Reading Books (From the Database)

Let's start with something simple: a version of Burt's Books that reads its list of books from the database. The first thing we'll need to do is create a database and a collection on our MongoDB server and populate it with book documents, like so:

```
>>> import pymongo
>>> conn = pymongo.Connection()
>>> db = conn["bookstore"]
>>> db.books.insert({
...     "title":"Programming Collective Intelligence",
...     "subtitle": "Building Smart Web 2.0 Applications",
...     "image":"/static/images/collective_intelligence.gif",
...     "author": "Toby Segaran",
...     "date_added":1310248056,
...     "date_released": "August 2007",
...     "isbn":"978-0-596-52932-1",
...     "description":"<p>[...]</p>"
... })
ObjectId('4eb6f1a6136fc42171000000')
>>> db.books.insert({
...     "title":"RESTful Web Services",
...     "subtitle": "Web services for the real world",
...     "image":"/static/images/restful_web_services.gif",
...     "author": "Leonard Richardson, Sam Ruby",
...     "date_added":1311148056,
...     "date_released": "May 2007",
```

```
...       "isbn":"978-0-596-52926-0",
...       "description":"<p>[...]</p>"
... })
ObjectId('4eb6f1cb136fc42171000001')
```

(We've omitted the descriptions of these books to save space.) Once we have these documents in the database, we're ready to roll. Example 4-3 shows the source code for the modified version of the Burt's Books web application, called *burts_books_db.py*.

Example 4-3. Reading from the database: burts_books_db.py

```python
import os.path
import tornado.auth
import tornado.escape
import tornado.httpserver
import tornado.ioloop
import tornado.options
import tornado.web
from tornado.options import define, options
import pymongo

define("port", default=8000, help="run on the given port", type=int)

class Application(tornado.web.Application):
    def __init__(self):
        handlers = [
            (r"/", MainHandler),
            (r"/recommended/", RecommendedHandler),
        ]
        settings = dict(
            template_path=os.path.join(os.path.dirname(__file__), "templates"),
            static_path=os.path.join(os.path.dirname(__file__), "static"),
            ui_modules={"Book": BookModule},
            debug=True,
            )
        conn = pymongo.Connection("localhost", 27017)
        self.db = conn["bookstore"]
        tornado.web.Application.__init__(self, handlers, **settings)

class MainHandler(tornado.web.RequestHandler):
    def get(self):
        self.render(
            "index.html",
            page_title = "Burt's Books | Home",
            header_text = "Welcome to Burt's Books!",
        )

class RecommendedHandler(tornado.web.RequestHandler):
    def get(self):
        coll = self.application.db.books
        books = coll.find()
        self.render(
            "recommended.html",
            page_title = "Burt's Books | Recommended Reading",
            header_text = "Recommended Reading",
```

```
            books = books
        )

class BookModule(tornado.web.UIModule):
    def render(self, book):
        return self.render_string(
            "modules/book.html",
            book=book,
        )
    def css_files(self):
        return "/static/css/recommended.css"
    def javascript_files(self):
        return "/static/js/recommended.js"

if __name__ == "__main__":
    tornado.options.parse_command_line()
    http_server = tornado.httpserver.HTTPServer(Application())
    http_server.listen(options.port)
    tornado.ioloop.IOLoop.instance().start()
```

As you can see, this program is almost exactly identical to the original Burt's Books web application presented in Chapter 3. There are two differences. First, we've added a db attribute to our Application connected to a MongoDB server:

```
conn = pymongo.Connection("localhost", 27017)
self.db = conn["bookstore"]
```

Second, we use the connection's find method to get a list of book documents from the database, and pass that list in when rendering *recommended.html* in the get method of RecommendedHandler. Here's the relevant code:

```
def get(self):
    coll = self.application.db.books
    books = coll.find()
    self.render(
        "recommended.html",
        page_title = "Burt's Books | Recommended Reading",
        header_text = "Recommended Reading",
        books = books
    )
```

Previously, the list of books had been hardcoded into the get method. However, because the documents we added to MongoDB have the same fields as the original hardcoded dictionaries, the template code we wrote works without any modification.

Run the application like so:

```
$ python burts_books_db.py
```

And then point your web browser to *http://localhost:8000/recommended/*. At this point, it should look almost exactly like the hardcoded version of Burt's Books (see Figure 3-6).

Editing and Adding Books

The next step is to make an interface for editing books that are already in the database, and to add new books to the database. In order to do this, we need to make a form for the user to fill out with book information, a handler to serve that form, and a handler to process the results of that form and put them in the database.

The source code for this version of Burt's Books is nearly identical to the code previously presented, with a few additions that we'll discuss below. You can follow along with the full source code that came with the book; the relevant program is *burts_books_rwdb.py*.

Rendering the edit form

Here's the source code for `BookEditHandler`, which performs two jobs:

1. A `GET` request to the handler renders an HTML form (in the template *book_edit.html*), potentially with data for an existing book.

2. A `POST` request to the handler takes data from the form and either updates an existing book record in the database, or adds a new one, depending on the data supplied.

Here's the source code for the handler:

```
class BookEditHandler(tornado.web.RequestHandler):
    def get(self, isbn=None):
        book = dict()
        if isbn:
            coll = self.application.db.books
            book = coll.find_one({"isbn": isbn})
        self.render("book_edit.html",
            page_title="Burt's Books",
            header_text="Edit book",
            book=book)

    def post(self, isbn=None):
        import time
        book_fields = ['isbn', 'title', 'subtitle', 'image', 'author',
            'date_released', 'description']
        coll = self.application.db.books
        book = dict()
        if isbn:
            book = coll.find_one({"isbn": isbn})
        for key in book_fields:
            book[key] = self.get_argument(key, None)

        if isbn:
            coll.save(book)
        else:
            book['date_added'] = int(time.time())
            coll.insert(book)
        self.redirect("/recommended/")
```

We'll talk about the details in a second, but first let's discuss how we've set up our Application class to route requests to this handler. Here's the relevant section from the Application's __init__ method:

```
handlers = [
    (r"/", MainHandler),
    (r"/recommended/", RecommendedHandler),
    (r"/edit/([0-9Xx\-]+)", BookEditHandler),
    (r"/add", BookEditHandler)
]
```

As you can see, BookEditHandler handles requests for *two different* path patterns. One of these, /add, serves up the edit form with no existing information, so you can add a new book to the database; the other, /edit/([0-9Xx\-]+), renders the form with information for a pre-existing book, according to the book's ISBN.

Retrieving book information from the database

Let's look at the get method in BookEditHandler to see how it works:

```
def get(self, isbn=None):
    book = dict()
    if isbn:
        coll = self.application.db.books
        book = coll.find_one({"isbn": isbn})
    self.render("book_edit.html",
        page_title="Burt's Books",
        header_text="Edit book",
        book=book)
```

If the method is invoked as a result of a request to /add, Tornado will call the get method without a second argument (as there's no corresponding group in the regular expression for the path). In this case, the default, an empty book dictionary is passed to the *book_edit.html* template.

If the method was called as a result of a request to, for example, /edit/0-123-456, the isbn parameter is set to the value 0-123-456. In this case, we get the books collection from our Application instance and use it to look up the book with the corresponding ISBN. Then we pass the resulting book dictionary into the template.

Here's the template (*book_edit.html*):

```
{% extends "main.html" %}
{% autoescape None %}

{% block body %}
<form method="POST">
    ISBN <input type="text" name="isbn"
        value="{{ book.get('isbn', '') }}"><br>
    Title <input type="text" name="title"
        value="{{ book.get('title', '') }}"><br>
    Subtitle <input type="text" name="subtitle"
        value="{{ book.get('subtitle', '') }}"><br>
    Image <input type="text" name="image"
```

```
            value="{{ book.get('image', '') }}"><br>
    Author <input type="text" name="author"
            value="{{ book.get('author', '') }}"><br>
    Date released <input type="text" name="date_released"
            value="{{ book.get('date_released', '') }}"><br>
    Description<br>
    <textarea name="description" rows="5"
            cols="40">{% raw book.get('description', '')%}</textarea><br>
    <input type="submit" value="Save">
</form>
{% end %}
```

This is a fairly conventional HTML form. We're using the book dictionary passed in from the request handler to prepopulate the form with data from the existing book, if any; we use the Python dictionary object's get method to supply a default value for a key if the key isn't present in the dictionary. Note that the name attributes of the input tags are set to the corresponding key of the book dictionary; this will make it easy to associate the data from the form with the data we want to put into the database.

Also note that, because the form tag lacks an action attribute, the form's POST will be directed to the current URL, which is precisely what we want (e.g., if the page was loaded as /edit/0-123-456, the POST request will go to /edit/0-123-456; if the page was loaded as /add, the POST will go to /add). Figure 4-1 shows what the page looks like when rendered.

Saving to the database

Let's take a look at the post method of BookEditHandler. This method handles requests that come from the book edit form. Here's the source code:

```
def post(self, isbn=None):
    import time
    book_fields = ['isbn', 'title', 'subtitle', 'image', 'author',
        'date_released', 'description']
    coll = self.application.db.books
    book = dict()
    if isbn:
        book = coll.find_one({"isbn": isbn})
    for key in book_fields:
        book[key] = self.get_argument(key, None)

    if isbn:
        coll.save(book)
    else:
        book['date_added'] = int(time.time())
        coll.insert(book)
    self.redirect("/recommended/")
```

Like the get method, the post method does double duty: it handles requests to edit existing documents and requests to add a new document. If there's an isbn argument (i.e., the path of the request was something like /edit/0-123-456), we assume that we're

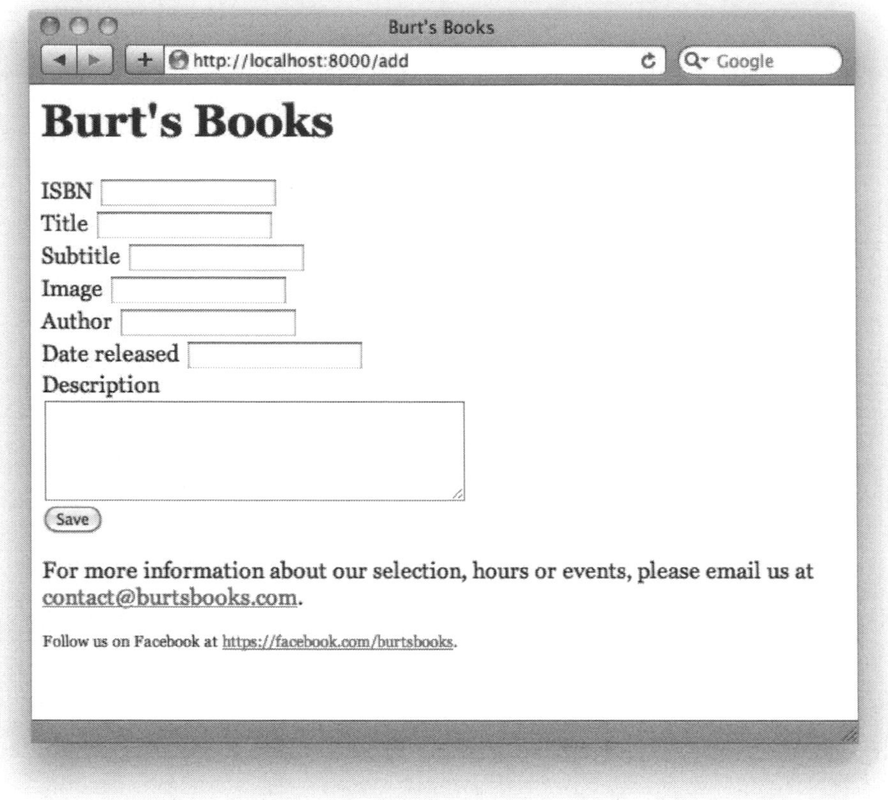

Figure 4-1. Burt's Books: Form for adding a new book

editing the document with the given ISBN. If such an argument is not present, we assume that we're adding a new document.

We begin with an empty dictionary variable called book. If we're editing an existing book, we load the document corresponding to the incoming ISBN from the database using the book collection's find_one method. In either case, the book_fields list specifies what fields should be present in a book document. We iterate over this list, grabbing the corresponding values from the POST request using the get_argument method of the RequestHandler object.

At this point, we're ready to update the database. If we have an ISBN, we call the collection's save method to update the book document in the database. If not, we call the collection's insert method, taking care to first add a value for the date_added key. (We didn't include this in our list of fields to fetch from the incoming request, as it doesn't make sense to be able to edit the date_added value after the book has been added to the database.) When we're done, we use the redirect method of the RequestHandler class to send the user back to the Recommendations page. Any changes that we made should be visible there immediately. Figure 4-2 shows what the updated Recommendations page might look like.

You'll also notice that we've added an "Edit" link to each book entry, which links to the Edit form for each book in the list. Here's the source code for the modified Book module:

```
<div class="book" style="overflow: auto">
    <h3 class="book_title">{{ book["title"] }}</h3>
    {% if book["subtitle"] != "" %}
        <h4 class="book_subtitle">{{ book["subtitle"] }}</h4>
    {% end %}
    <img src="{{ book["image"] }}" class="book_image"/>
    <div class="book_details">
        <div class="book_date_released">Released: {{ book["date_released"]}}</div>
        <div class="book_date_added">Added: {{ locale.format_date(book["date_added"],
relative=False) }}</div>
        <h5>Description:</h5>
        <div class="book_body">{% raw book["description"] %}</div>
        <p><a href="/edit/{{ book['isbn'] }}">Edit</a></p>
    </div>
</div>
```

The important line is this one:

```
<p><a href="/edit/{{ book['isbn'] }}">Edit</a></p>
```

The link to the Edit page is made by appending the value of the book's `isbn` key to the string `/edit/`. This link will lead to the Edit form for the book in question. You can see the results in Figure 4-3.

MongoDB: Next Steps

We've covered only the bare essentials of MongoDB here—just enough to implement the example web applications in this chapter. If you're interested in learning more about PyMongo and MongoDB in general, the PyMongo tutorial (*http://api.mongodb.org/python/2.0.1/tutorial.html*) and the MongoDB tutorial (*http://www.mongodb.org/display/DOCS/Tutorial*) are good places to start.

If you're interested in making MongoDB applications with Tornado that perform well at scale, you'll want to familiarize yourself with asyncmongo (*https://github.com/bitly/asyncmongo*), a PyMongo-like library for performing MongoDB requests asynchronously. We'll discuss what asynchronous requests are, and why they're good for scalable web applications, in Chapter 5.

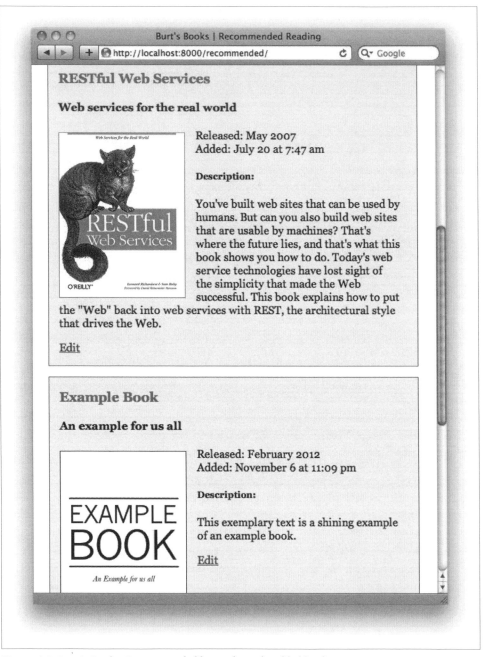

Figure 4-2. Burt's Books: Recommended list with newly added book

Figure 4-3. Burt's Books: Recommended list with edit links

Asynchronous Web Services

Thus far, we've taken a look at many of the features that make Tornado such a powerful framework for web applications. Its simplicity, ease of use, and handy helpers are enough reason to make it a great choice for many web projects. However, one of the most talked about features of Tornado is its ability to fetch and serve content asynchronously, and with good reason: it makes it easy to handle nonblocking requests, ultimately resulting in more efficient processes and greater scaling possibilities. In this chapter, we'll take a look at the basics of asynchronous requests in Tornado, as well as some long polling techniques that will allow you to write simpler web applications that can serve more requests with fewer resources.

Asynchronous Web Requests

Most web applications (including the examples we've looked at thus far) are blocking in nature, meaning that while a request is being handled, the process hangs until the request is completed. In most cases, web requests handled by Tornado should complete fast enough that this is not a concern. However, for operations that can take some time to complete (like large database requests or calls to external APIs) it means that the application is effectively locked until the process is finished, and for obvious reasons that is a problem at scale.

However, Tornado gives us better ways to handle this sort of situation. Instead of leaving a process hanging while it waits for a request to finish, the application can start a request and give it a callback for when that completes, leaving the I/O loop open to serve other clients while it waits for the first process to complete.

To illustrate Tornado's asynchronous features, we're going to build a simple web application that makes HTTP requests to the Twitter Search API. The web application takes a parameter q on the query string and determines how often a tweet with that search term is posted on Twitter ("tweets per second"). The methodology for determining this number is very rough, but it's good enough for example purposes. Figure 5-1 shows what the application looks like.

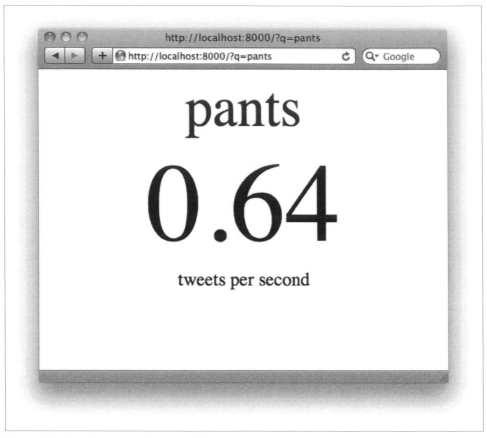

Figure 5-1. Asynchronous HTTP example: tweet rate

We're going to show three versions of this application: first, the version that uses a synchronous HTTP request, then a version that uses Tornado's asynchronous HTTP client with a callback. Finally, we'll show how to use Tornado 2.1's new gen module to make asynchronous HTTP requests cleaner and easier to implement. You don't need to be an expert on the Twitter Search API to understand some examples, but a passing familiarity won't hurt. You can read the developer documentation for the search API here: *https://dev.twitter.com/docs/api/1/get/search*.

Starting Synchronous

Example 5-1 contains the source code for the synchronous version of our tweet rate calculator. Note that we import Tornado's httpclient module up at the top: we're going to use the HTTPClient class from that module to perform our HTTP requests. Later on, we'll use the AsyncHTTPClient class, which is available in the same module.

Example 5-1. Synchronous HTTP requests: tweet_rate.py

```python
import tornado.httpserver
import tornado.ioloop
import tornado.options
import tornado.web
import tornado.httpclient

import urllib
import json
import datetime
import time

from tornado.options import define, options
define("port", default=8000, help="run on the given port", type=int)

class IndexHandler(tornado.web.RequestHandler):
    def get(self):
        query = self.get_argument('q')
        client = tornado.httpclient.HTTPClient()
        response = client.fetch("http://search.twitter.com/search.json?" + \
                urllib.urlencode({"q": query, "result_type": "recent", "rpp": 100}))
        body = json.loads(response.body)
        result_count = len(body['results'])
        now = datetime.datetime.utcnow()
        raw_oldest_tweet_at = body['results'][-1]['created_at']
        oldest_tweet_at = datetime.datetime.strptime(raw_oldest_tweet_at,
                "%a, %d %b %Y %H:%M:%S +0000")
        seconds_diff = time.mktime(now.timetuple()) - \
                time.mktime(oldest_tweet_at.timetuple())
        tweets_per_second = float(result_count) / seconds_diff
        self.write("""
<div style="text-align: center">
    <div style="font-size: 72px">%s</div>
    <div style="font-size: 144px">%.02f</div>
    <div style="font-size: 24px">tweets per second</div>
</div>""" % (query, tweets_per_second))

if __name__ == "__main__":
    tornado.options.parse_command_line()
    app = tornado.web.Application(handlers=[(r"/", IndexHandler)])
    http_server = tornado.httpserver.HTTPServer(app)
    http_server.listen(options.port)
    tornado.ioloop.IOLoop.instance().start()
```

The structure of this program should be familiar to you by now: we have a `RequestHandler` class, `IndexHandler`, that handles requests going to the root path of the application. Inside the `get` method of `IndexHandler`, we grab the q parameter from the query string (using `get_argument`) and then use it to perform a request to the Twitter Search API. Here's the most relevant bit of code:

```python
client = tornado.httpclient.HTTPClient()
response = client.fetch("http://search.twitter.com/search.json?" + \
        urllib.urlencode({"q": query, "result_type": "recent", "rpp": 100}))
body = json.loads(response.body)
```

Here we instantiate Tornado's `HTTPClient` class, then call `fetch` on the resulting object. The synchronous version of `fetch` method takes as a parameter the URL to be fetched. We construct a URL to grab relevant search results from the Twitter Search API (the `rpp` parameter specifies that we want 100 tweets in the first page of search results, while the `result_type` parameter specifies that we want only the most recent tweets that match our search). The `fetch` method returns an `HTTPResponse` object, whose `body` attribute contains whatever data was fetched from the remote URL. Twitter returns results in JSON format, so we use Python's `json` module to create a Python data structure from the results.

 The `HTTPResponse` object that the `fetch` method returns allows you to access all parts of the HTTP response, not just the body. Read more about it in the official documentation (*http://www.tornadoweb.org/doc umentation/httpclient.html*).

The rest of the code in the handler is concerned with calculating our tweets per second figure. We use the difference in time between the oldest tweet in the search results and the current timestamp to determine how many seconds the search covers, then use that number to divide the number of tweets retrieved in the search to arrive at our final figure. Finally, we write some rudimentary HTML with the figure to the browser.

The Trouble with Blocking

So far, we've written a simple Tornado application that makes a request to the Twitter API and then returns the results to the browser. And while the application itself should be fairly quick to respond, there will always be a lag between when the request to Twitter is made and when the search data returns. In a synchronous (and for now, we'll assume single-threaded) application, this means that only one request can be served at a time. So, if your application involves a two-second API request, you're going to be serving (at most!) one request every other second. That's not what you might call a highly scalable application, even spread over multiple threads and/or multiple servers.

To take a concrete look at this, let's benchmark the example we've written. You can verify the performance of this application with any benchmarking tool, though in this case we'll be utilizing the excellent Siege utility (*http://www.joedog.org/index/siege -home*) for our tests. It can be used like this:

```
$ siege http://localhost:8000/?q=pants -c10 -t10s
```

In this case, Siege will make roughly 10 concurrent requests for 10 seconds to our application, the output of which is shown in Figure 5-2. The problem, as we can quickly see here, is that while each request returns somewhat quickly on its own, the API roundtrip has enough lag in it that it forces the process to hang until the request completes and the data is handled. This is not a concern for just one or two requests, but spread across 100 (or even 10) users, it means slowdowns across the board.

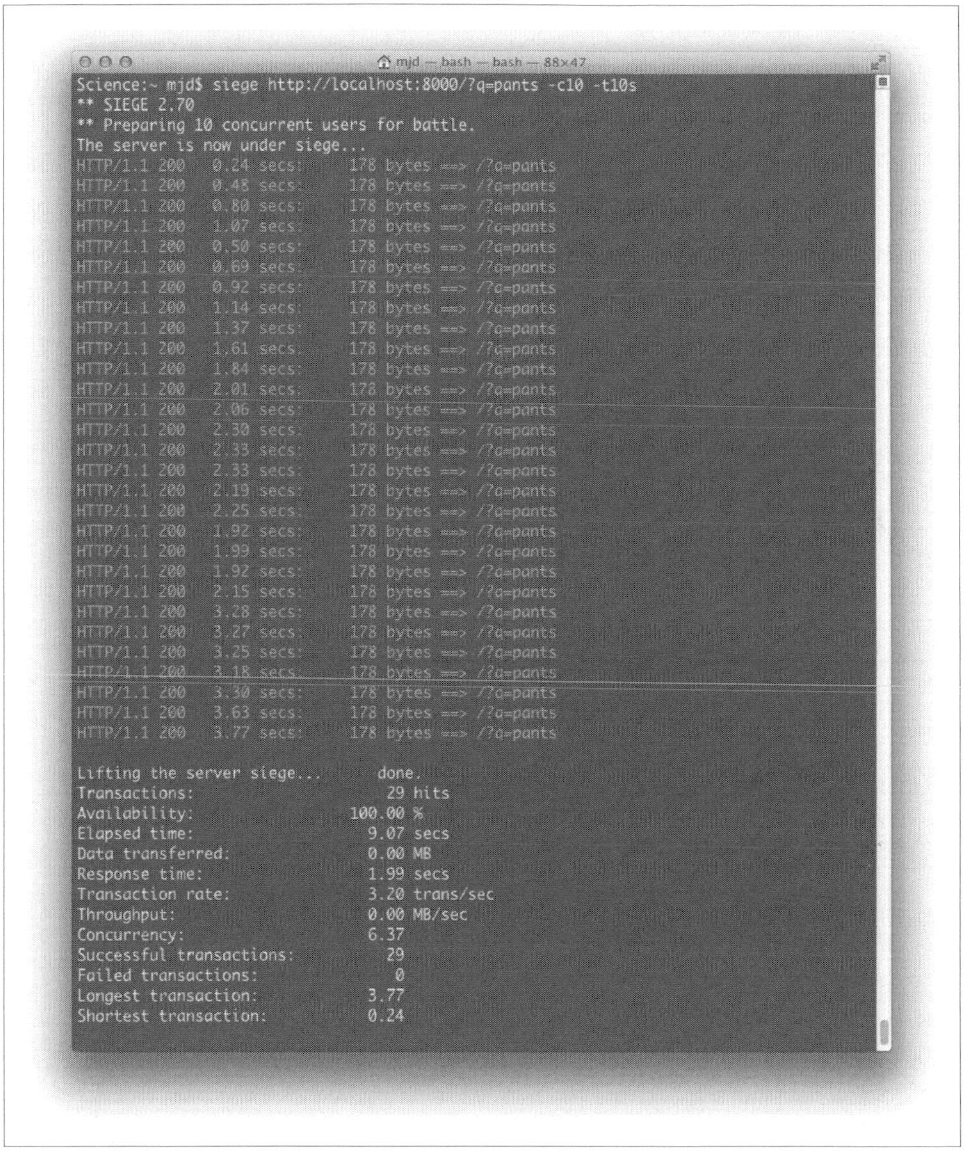

Figure 5-2. Synchronous tweet-rate fetch

Here, 10 simulated users over a time period of fewer than 10 seconds brought the average response time to 1.99 seconds, with a grand total of 29 hits served. And keep in mind, this example is serving just a dead-simple web page. If you were to add in calls to other web services or databases, the result would be far worse. If this type of code were used on a site that got even a moderate amount of traffic, requests would get increasingly slower, and eventually begin to time out or fail.

Basic Asynchronous Calls

Fortunately, Tornado includes a class called `AsyncHTTPClient`, which performs HTTP requests asynchronously. It works a lot like the synchronous client illustrated in Example 5-1, with a few important differences that we'll discuss. See Example 5-2 for the source code.

Example 5-2. Asynchronous HTTP requests: tweet_rate_async.py

```python
import tornado.httpserver
import tornado.ioloop
import tornado.options
import tornado.web
import tornado.httpclient

import urllib
import json
import datetime
import time

from tornado.options import define, options
define("port", default=8000, help="run on the given port", type=int)

class IndexHandler(tornado.web.RequestHandler):
    @tornado.web.asynchronous
    def get(self):
        query = self.get_argument('q')
        client = tornado.httpclient.AsyncHTTPClient()
        client.fetch("http://search.twitter.com/search.json?" + \
                urllib.urlencode({"q": query, "result_type": "recent", "rpp": 100}),
                callback=self.on_response)

    def on_response(self, response):
        body = json.loads(response.body)
        result_count = len(body['results'])
        now = datetime.datetime.utcnow()
        raw_oldest_tweet_at = body['results'][-1]['created_at']
        oldest_tweet_at = datetime.datetime.strptime(raw_oldest_tweet_at,
                "%a, %d %b %Y %H:%M:%S +0000")
        seconds_diff = time.mktime(now.timetuple()) - \
                time.mktime(oldest_tweet_at.timetuple())
        tweets_per_second = float(result_count) / seconds_diff
        self.write("""
<div style="text-align: center">
    <div style="font-size: 72px">%s</div>
    <div style="font-size: 144px">%.02f</div>
    <div style="font-size: 24px">tweets per second</div>
</div>""" % (self.get_argument('q'), tweets_per_second))
        self.finish()

if __name__ == "__main__":
    tornado.options.parse_command_line()
    app = tornado.web.Application(handlers=[(r"/", IndexHandler)])
    http_server = tornado.httpserver.HTTPServer(app)
```

```
http_server.listen(options.port)
tornado.ioloop.IOLoop.instance().start()
```

The `fetch` method of `AsyncHTTPClient` does not return with the results of the call. Instead, it specifies a `callback` parameter; the method or function you specify will be called when the HTTP request is complete, with the `HTTPResponse` object as a parameter.

```
client = tornado.httpclient.AsyncHTTPClient()
client.fetch("http://search.twitter.com/search.json?" + »
urllib.urlencode({"q": query, "result_type": "recent", "rpp": 100}),
        callback=self.on_response)
```

In this example, we specified the method `on_response` as the callback. All of the logic that we used to transform the Twitter Search API request into a web page with the desired output was then moved into the `on_response` function. Also note the use of the `@tornado.web.asynchronous` decorator (before the definition of the `get` method) and the call to `self.finish()` at the end of the callback method. We'll discuss those in more detail shortly.

This version of the application has the same outward behavior as the synchronous version, but it performs much better. How much better? Well, let's look at the benchmark readout.

As you can see in Figure 5-3, we've gone from 3.20 transactions per second in our synchronous example to 12.59, serving a total of 118 hits for the same period of time. That's a pretty solid improvement! As you could imagine, spread over more users and a longer period of time, this would serve many more connections, and would not be as likely to suffer the slowdown issues that the synchronous example showed.

The asynchronous Decorator and the finish Method

Tornado's default behavior is to close the connection to the client when the function handling the request returns. In normal circumstances, this is exactly what you want. But when we're performing an asynchronous request that requires a callback, we need the connection to stay open until the callback has been executed. You can tell Tornado to leave the connection open by using the `@tornado.web.asynchronous` decorator on the method whose behavior you want to change, as we did with the `get` method of the `IndexHandler` in the asynchronous version of the Tweet Rate example. The following is the relevant snippet of code:

```
class IndexHandler(tornado.web.RequestHandler):
    @tornado.web.asynchronous
    def get(self):
        query = self.get_argument('q')
        [... other request handler code here...]
```

Note that when you use the `@tornado.web.asynchronous` decorator, Tornado will never close the connection on its own. You must explicitly tell Tornado to close the request by calling the `finish` method of your `RequestHandler` object. (Otherwise, the request

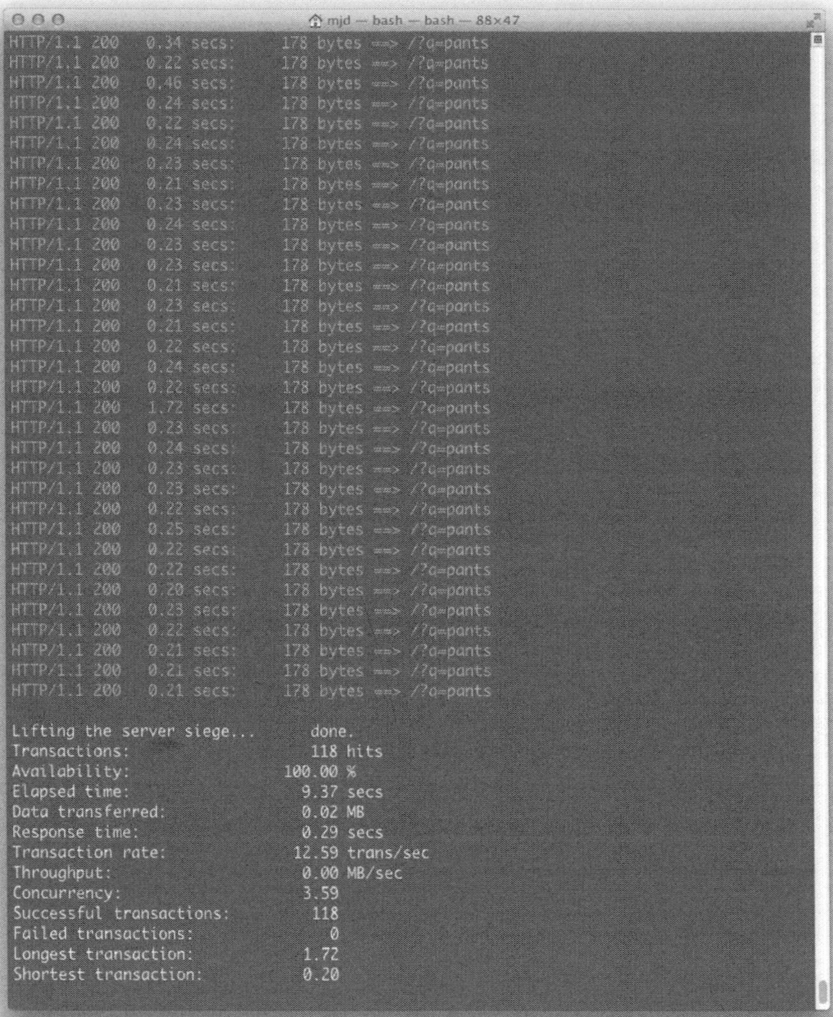

Figure 5-3. Asynchronous tweet-rate fetch

will appear to hang, and the browser may or may not display the data we've already sent to the client.) In the preceding asynchronous example, we called the `finish` method right after our call to `write` in the `on_response` function:

```
[... other callback code ...]
    self.write("""
<div style="text-align: center">
    <div style="font-size: 72px">%s</div>
```

```
    <div style="font-size: 144px">%.02f</div>
    <div style="font-size: 24px">tweets per second</div>
</div>""" % (self.get_argument('q'), tweets_per_second))
        self.finish()
```

Asynchronous Generators

Now, the asynchronous version of our Tweet Rate program works great and performs well. Unfortunately, it's a little bit messy: we've had to split our code for handling the request across two different methods. This can get especially hard to code and maintain when we have two or more asynchronous requests to perform, each dependent on the previous call: soon you can find yourself calling callbacks from within callbacks within callbacks. What follows is a contrived (but not impossible) illustration:

```
def get(self):
    client = AsyncHTTPClient()
    client.fetch("http://example.com", callback=on_response)

def on_response(self, response):
    client = AsyncHTTPClient()
    client.fetch("http://another.example.com/", callback=on_response2)

def on_response2(self, response):
    client = AsyncHTTPClient()
    client.fetch("http://still.another.example.com/", callback=on_response3)

def on_response3(self, response):
    [etc., etc.]
```

Fortunately, Tornado 2.1 introduced the tornado.gen module, which provides a cleaner pattern for performing asynchronous requests. Example 5-3 contains the source code for a version of the Tweet Rate application that uses tornado.gen. Take a look, and then we'll discuss how it works.

Example 5-3. Asynchronous requests with the generator pattern: tweet_rate_gen.py

```
import tornado.httpserver
import tornado.ioloop
import tornado.options
import tornado.web
import tornado.httpclient
import tornado.gen

import urllib
import json
import datetime
import time

from tornado.options import define, options
define("port", default=8000, help="run on the given port", type=int)

class IndexHandler(tornado.web.RequestHandler):
    @tornado.web.asynchronous
```

```
    @tornado.gen.engine
    def get(self):
        query = self.get_argument('q')
        client = tornado.httpclient.AsyncHTTPClient()
        response = yield tornado.gen.Task(client.fetch,
                "http://search.twitter.com/search.json?" + \
                urllib.urlencode({"q": query, "result_type": "recent", "rpp": 100}))
        body = json.loads(response.body)
        result_count = len(body['results'])
        now = datetime.datetime.utcnow()
        raw_oldest_tweet_at = body['results'][-1]['created_at']
        oldest_tweet_at = datetime.datetime.strptime(raw_oldest_tweet_at,
                "%a, %d %b %Y %H:%M:%S +0000")
        seconds_diff = time.mktime(now.timetuple()) - \
                time.mktime(oldest_tweet_at.timetuple())
        tweets_per_second = float(result_count) / seconds_diff
        self.write("""
<div style="text-align: center">
    <div style="font-size: 72px">%s</div>
    <div style="font-size: 144px">%.02f</div>
    <div style="font-size: 24px">tweets per second</div>
</div>""" % (query, tweets_per_second))
        self.finish()

if __name__ == "__main__":
    tornado.options.parse_command_line()
    app = tornado.web.Application(handlers=[(r"/", IndexHandler)])
    http_server = tornado.httpserver.HTTPServer(app)
    http_server.listen(options.port)
    tornado.ioloop.IOLoop.instance().start()
```

As you can see, this code here is largely identical to the previous two versions of the
code. The main difference is in how we call the `fetch` method of the `AsyncHTTPClient`
object. Here's the relevant part of the code:

```
        client = tornado.httpclient.AsyncHTTPClient()
        response = yield tornado.gen.Task(client.fetch,
                "http://search.twitter.com/search.json?" + \
                urllib.urlencode({"q": query, "result_type": "recent", "rpp": 100}))
        body = json.loads(response.body)
```

We use Python's `yield` keyword and an instance of the `tornado.gen.Task` object, passing
in the function we want to call and the parameters to pass to that function. Here, the
use of `yield` returns control of the program to Tornado, allowing it to perform other
tasks while the HTTP request is in progress. When the HTTP request is finished, the
`RequestHandler` method resumes where it left off. The beauty of this construction is that
it returns the HTTP response right in the request handler, not in a callback. As a con-
sequence, the code is easier to understand: all of the logic related to the request is
located in the same place. The HTTP request is still performed asynchronously, however, and so we get the same performance gains from using `tornado.gen` as we do from
using an asynchronous request with a callback, as we can see in Figure 5-4.

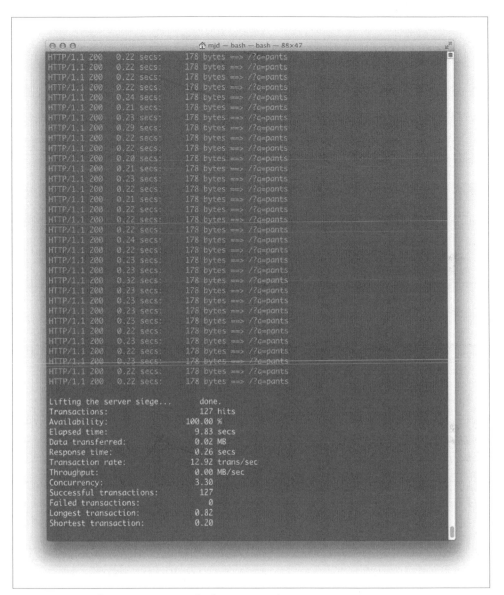

Figure 5-4. Asynchronous tweet-rate fetch using tornado.gen

Note the use of the @tornado.gen.engine decorator just before the definition of the get method; this is what informs Tornado that the method will be using the tornado.gen.Task class. The tornado.gen module has a number of other classes and functions that ease asynchronous programming in Tornado. It's worth looking over the documentation (*http://www.tornadoweb.org/documentation/gen.html*).

> ## Making Everything Asynchronous
>
> We've been using Tornado's asynchronous HTTP client in this chapter as an illustration of how to perform tasks asynchronously. Other developers have written asynchronous client libraries for other kinds of tasks. Volunteers maintain a fairly complete list of such libraries on the Tornado wiki (*https://github.com/facebook/tornado/wiki/Links*).
>
> One notable example is bit.ly's asyncmongo (*https://github.com/bitly/asyncmongo*), which can be used to make calls to a MongoDB server asynchronous. This one is particularly good choice for us, as it was developed specifically to provide async database access to Tornado developers, but for those using other databases, there's a good chance your data store of choice also has an asynchronous library listed there.

Summary of Asynchronous Operations

As we've seen in the preceding examples, asynchronous web services in Tornado are both easy to implement and incredibly powerful in practice. Using asynchronous handlers for longer API and database requests can keep your application from blocking, and ultimately serve more requests faster. While not every handler benefits from being asynchronous—and in fact trying to make a full application nonblocking can overcomplicate things quickly—Tornado's nonblocking features can be extremely handy for building web applications that depend on slower queries or external services.

However, it's worth noting here that these examples are fairly contrived. If you were designing an application with this functionality at any kind of scale, you'd probably want to have the client web browser do the Twitter search request (in JavaScript), and let the web server move on to serving other requests. In most cases, you'd at least want to cache the results so that two requests for the same search term didn't incur a full request to the remote API. In general, if you're doing an HTTP request on the backend just to serve your web content, you're probably going to want to rethink how your application is set up.

With this in mind, over the next set of examples we're going to take a look at dealing with asynchronous applications from the frontend side using tools like JavaScript to let the clients take on more of the work and help scale out your applications.

Long Polling with Tornado

Another advantage of Tornado's asynchronous architecture is the ease with which it handles HTTP long polling. This is a way of handling real-time updates, which can be used for effects as simple as a notification badge and as complex as multi-user chat rooms.

Developing web applications that offer real-time updates is a constant challenge for web programmers. Updating a user's status, sending new message notifications, or indicating any other global activity all require a method for the server to send messages to the browser after the initial document has finished loading. One early approach was for the browser to poll the server for new updates at a regular interval. This technique poses obvious challenges: the polling frequency must be fast enough that notifications are up-to-date, but not too frequent that the HTTP requests pose serious scaling challenges when hundreds or thousands of clients continually open new connections. Frequent polling presents a "death by a thousand cuts" strain on a web server.

So-called "server push" technology allows web applications to distribute updates in real time while maintaining reasonable resource usage and ensuring predictable scaling. For a server push technology to be practical, it must play nicely with existing browsers. The most popular technique is to emulate a server pushing updates by letting the browser initiate the connection. These sorts of HTTP connections are called long polling, or Comet requests.

Long polling means that the browser simply initiates an HTTP request whose connection the server intentionally leaves open. The browser will simply wait for the server to "push" a response whenever an update is available. After the server sends a response and closes the connection, (or if the client request times out on the browser side) the client simply opens a new connection and waits for the next update.

This section will cover HTTP long polling in a simple real-time application and demonstrate how Tornado's architecture makes these applications easy.

The Benefits of Long Polling

The primary appeal of HTTP long polling is that it dramatically reduces the load on a web server. Instead of clients making many short, frequent requests (and incurring the overhead of processing the HTTP headers each time), the server processes the connection only when it receives an initial request and again when there's a response to be sent. During the majority of the time that there's no new data, the connection won't consume any processor resources.

Browser compatibility is another huge benefit. Any web browser that supports AJAX requests can make long polling requests. No browser plug-ins or other add-ons are required. Compared with other server-push techniques, HTTP long polling ends up being one of the few viable options that are seen in widespread use.

We've already touched on some of the uses for long polling. In fact, the previously mentioned status updates, message notifications, and chat messages are all features on current popular web sites. Sites such as Google Docs use long polling for synchronized collaboration, where two people can edit a document simultaneously and watch each other's changes. Twitter uses long polling instruct the browser to display notifications that new status updates are available. Facebook uses the technique for its chat feature.

One reason long polling is so popular is that it improves an application's user experience: visitors no longer have to constantly refresh the page to see the latest content.

Example: Live Inventory Reporting

This example demonstrates a service that keeps a live count of a retailer's inventory updated across multiple shoppers' browsers. The application serves an HTML book detail page with an "Add to Cart" button and a count of the book's remaining inventory. Immediately after one shopper adds the book to her cart, other visitors browsing the site will see the remaining inventory decrement.

In order to provide the inventory updates, we need to write a RequestHandler subclass that doesn't immediately close the HTTP connection after the initial handler method is called. We accomplish this feat with Tornado's built-in asynchronous decorator, which we introduce in Example 5-4.

Example 5-4. Long polling: shopping_cart.py

```python
import tornado.web
import tornado.httpserver
import tornado.ioloop
import tornado.options
from uuid import uuid4

class ShoppingCart(object):
    totalInventory = 10
    callbacks = []
    carts = {}

    def register(self, callback):
        self.callbacks.append(callback)

    def moveItemToCart(self, session):
        if session in self.carts:
            return

        self.carts[session] = True
        self.notifyCallbacks()

    def removeItemFromCart(self, session):
        if session not in self.carts:
            return

        del(self.carts[session])
        self.notifyCallbacks()

    def notifyCallbacks(self):
        for c in self.callbacks:
            self.callbackHelper(c)

        self.callbacks = []
```

```python
    def callbackHelper(self, callback):
        callback(self.getInventoryCount())

    def getInventoryCount(self):
        return self.totalInventory - len(self.carts)

class DetailHandler(tornado.web.RequestHandler):
    def get(self):
        session = uuid4()
        count = self.application.shoppingCart.getInventoryCount()
        self.render("index.html", session=session, count=count)

class CartHandler(tornado.web.RequestHandler):
    def post(self):
        action = self.get_argument('action')
        session = self.get_argument('session')

        if not session:
            self.set_status(400)
            return

        if action == 'add':
            self.application.shoppingCart.moveItemToCart(session)
        elif action == 'remove':
            self.application.shoppingCart.removeItemFromCart(session)
        else:
            self.set_status(400)

class StatusHandler(tornado.web.RequestHandler):
    @tornado.web.asynchronous
    def get(self):
        self.application.shoppingCart.register(self.async_callback(self.on_message))

    def on_message(self, count):
        self.write('{"inventoryCount":"%d"}' % count)
        self.finish()

class Application(tornado.web.Application):
    def __init__(self):
        self.shoppingCart = ShoppingCart()

        handlers = [
            (r'/', DetailHandler),
            (r'/cart', CartHandler),
            (r'/cart/status', StatusHandler)
        ]

        settings = {
            'template_path': 'templates',
            'static_path': 'static'
        }

        tornado.web.Application.__init__(self, handlers, **settings)

if __name__ == '__main__':
```

```
tornado.options.parse_command_line()

app = Application()
server = tornado.httpserver.HTTPServer(app)
server.listen(8000)
tornado.ioloop.IOLoop.instance().start()
```

Let's take a closer look at *shopping_cart.py* before looking at the template and script files. We define a `ShoppingCart` class that maintains the number of items in our inventory and a list of the shoppers who have added the item to their carts. Next, we specify the `DetailHandler`, which renders the HTML; the `CartHandler`, which provides an interface to manipulate the cart; and the `StatusHandler`, which we query for notifications of changes to the global inventory.

The `DetailHandler` simply generates a unique identifier for each request of the page, provides the inventory count at the time of the request, and renders the *index.html* template to the browser. The `CartHandler` provides an API for the browser to request the item be added or removed from the visitor's shopping cart. The JavaScript running in the browser will submit `POST` requests to manipulate the visitor's cart. We will see how these methods interact with the inventory count queries that follow when we look at the `StatusHandler` and the `ShoppingCart` classes.

```
class StatusHandler(tornado.web.RequestHandler):
    @tornado.web.asynchronous
    def get(self):
        self.application.shoppingCart.register(self.async_callback(self.on_message))
```

The first thing to notice about the `StatusHandler` is the `@tornado.web.asynchronous` decorator on the get method. This instructs Tornado not to close the connection when the get method returns. In the method itself, we simply register a callback with the shopping cart controller. We wrap the callback method with `self.async_callback` to ensure that exceptions raised in the callback don't prevent the `RequestHandler` from properly closing the connection.

In Tornado versions prior to 1.1, callbacks had to be wrapped in the `self.async_callback()` method to catch any exceptions that might be thrown in the wrapped function. In Tornado versions 1.1 and newer, however, this is not explicitly necessary.

```
def on_message(self, count):
    self.write('{"inventoryCount":"%d"}' % count)
    self.finish()
```

Whenever a visitor's cart is manipulated, the `ShoppingCart` controller invokes the `on_message` method for each of the registered callbacks. This method writes the current inventory count to the client and closes the connection. (If the server doesn't close the connection, the browser may not know the request has completed, and won't notify the script that there's been an update.) Now that the long polling connections are closed, the shopping cart controller must remove the callbacks from the list of registered callbacks. In this example, we simply replace the list of callbacks with a new, empty list.

It is important to remove registered callbacks after they have been invoked and finished in the request handler, since invoking the callback subsequently would call `finish()` on a previously closed connection, which is an error.

Finally, the `ShoppingCart` controller manages inventory allocation and status callbacks. The `StatusHandler` registers callbacks via the `register` method, which appends the method to the internal `callbacks` array.

```python
def moveItemToCart(self, session):
    if session in self.carts:
        return

    self.carts[session] = True
    self.notifyCallbacks()

def removeItemFromCart(self, session):
    if session not in self.carts:
        return

    del(self.carts[session])
    self.notifyCallbacks()
```

The `ShoppingCart` controller also makes `addItemToCart` and `removeItemFromCart` methods available to the `CartHandler`. When the `CartHandler` invokes these methods, the requesting page's unique identifier (the `session` variable passed to the methods) is used to mark the inventory before we call `notifyCallbacks`.

```python
def notifyCallbacks(self):
    self.callbacks[:] = [c for c in self.callbacks if self.callbackHelper(c)]

def callbackHelper(self, callback):
    callback(self.getInventoryCount())
    return False
```

The registered callbacks are invoked with the current available inventory count and the callback list is emptied to ensure a callback isn't invoked on a closed connection.

See Example 5-5 for the HTML template that displays the list of books as they change.

Example 5-5. Long polling: index.html

```html
<html>
    <head>
        <title>Burt's Books &ndash; Book Detail</title>
        <script src="//ajax.googleapis.com/ajax/libs/jquery/1.7.1/jquery.min.js"
            type="text/javascript"></script>
        <script src="{{ static_url('scripts/inventory.js') }}"
            type="application/javascript"></script>
    </head>

    <body>
        <div>
```

```
        <h1>Burt's Books</h1>

        <hr/>

        <p><h2>The Definitive Guide to the Internet</h2>
        <em>Anonymous</em></p>
    </div>

    <img src="static/images/internet.jpg" alt="The Definitive Guide to the Internet" />

    <hr />

    <input type="hidden" id="session" value="{{ session }}" />
    <div id="add-to-cart">
        <p><span style="color: red;">Only <span id="count">{{ count }}</span>
            left in stock! Order now!</span></p>
        <p>$20.00 <input type="submit" value="Add to Cart" id="add-button" /></p>
    </div>
    <div id="remove-from-cart" style="display: none;">
        <p><span style="color: green;">One copy is in your cart.</p>
        <p><input type="submit" value="Remove from Cart" id="remove-button" /></p>
    </div>
    </body>
</html>
```

When the `DetailHandler` renders the *index.html* template, we simply render the book description and include the required JavaScript code. Additionally, we dynamically include a unique ID via the `session` variable and the current inventory stock as `count`.

Finally, we will discuss the client-side JavaScript code. While this is a book on Tornado, and therefore we've been using Python up until now, the client-side code is vital enough to this example that it's important to at least understand the gist of it. In Example 5-6, we're using the jQuery library to assist in defining the page's behavior in the browser.

Example 5-6. Long polling: inventory.js

```
$(document).ready(function() {
    document.session = $('#session').val();

    setTimeout(requestInventory, 100);

    $('#add-button').click(function(event) {
        jQuery.ajax({
            url: '//localhost:8000/cart',
            type: 'POST',
            data: {
                session: document.session,
                action: 'add'
            },
            dataType: 'json',
            beforeSend: function(xhr, settings) {
                $(event.target).attr('disabled', 'disabled');
            },
```

```
            success: function(data, status, xhr) {
                $('#add-to-cart').hide();
                $('#remove-from-cart').show();
                $(event.target).removeAttr('disabled');
            }
        });
    });

    $('#remove-button').click(function(event) {
        jQuery.ajax({
            url: '//localhost:8000/cart',
            type: 'POST',
            data: {
                session: document.session,
                action: 'remove'
            },
            dataType: 'json',
            beforeSend: function(xhr, settings) {
                $(event.target).attr('disabled', 'disabled');
            },
            success: function(data, status, xhr) {
                $('#remove-from-cart').hide();
                $('#add-to-cart').show();
                $(event.target).removeAttr('disabled');
            }
        });
    });
});

function requestInventory() {
    jQuery.getJSON('//localhost:8000/cart/status', {session: document.session},
        function(data, status, xhr) {
            $('#count').html(data['inventoryCount']);
            setTimeout(requestInventory, 0);
        }
    );
}
```

When the document is finished loading, we add click event handlers to the "Add to Cart" button as well as the hidden "Remove from Cart" button. These event handler functions make the associated API calls to the server and swap the add-to-cart interface for the remove-from-cart one.

```
function requestInventory() {
    jQuery.getJSON('//localhost:8000/cart/status', {session: document.session},
        function(data, status, xhr) {
            $('#count').html(data['inventoryCount']);
            setTimeout(requestInventory, 0);
        }
    );
}
```

The requestInventory function is called with a short delay after the page has finished loading. In the function body, we initiate the long polling connection via an HTTP

GET request to the /cart/status resource. The delay allows the loading progress indicator to complete when the browser finishes rendering the page and prevents the Esc key or Stop button from interrupting the long polling request. When the request returns successfully, the content of the count span is updated with the current stock tally. Figure 5-5 shows two browser windows displaying full inventory.

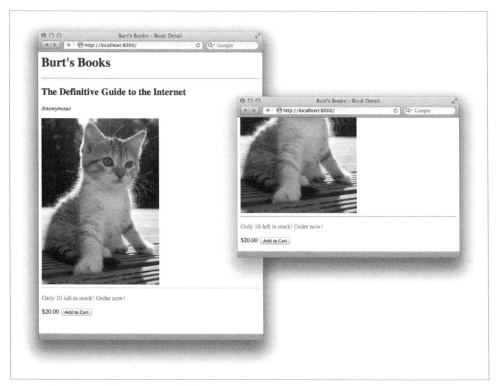

Figure 5-5. Long polling example: Full inventory

Now, when you run the server, you will be able to load the root URL and see the current inventory count for the book. Open multiple browser windows to the detail page and click the "Add to Cart" button in one of the windows. The number of remaining copies will immediately be updated in the other windows, as illustrated in Figure 5-6.

This is a somewhat naive shopping cart implementation, to be sure—there is no logic to make sure we don't dip below our total stock, not to mention that the data will not persist between invocations of the Tornado application or between parallel instances of the application on the same server. We will leave those improvements as an exercise for the reader.

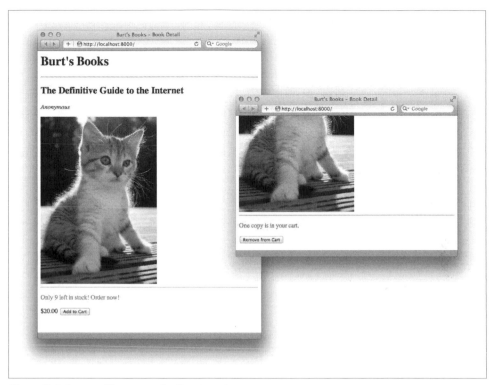

Figure 5-6. Long polling example: One item in a cart

The Downsides of Long Polling

As we've seen, HTTP long polling is incredibly useful for communicating highly interactive feedback about a site or a particular user's status. But there are a couple of pitfalls to be aware of.

When developing applications that use long polling, it's important to remember that the server has no control over the browser's request timeout interval. It's up to the browser to re-initiate the HTTP connection in the case of any interruption. Another potential issue is that many web browsers limit the number of simultaneous requests that may be opened to a particular host. With one connection sitting idle, the number of requests remaining to download site content may be limited.

Additionally, you should still be aware of how the requests will affect server performance. Consider the shopping cart application again. Since all of the Comet requests are answered and closed *en masse* whenever the inventory changes, the server will be slammed with new requests as browsers re-establish the connections. For applications like user-to-user chat or message notifications, where only a few users' connections will close at a time, this is less of an issue.

WebSockets with Tornado

WebSockets are a new protocol for client-server communication proposed in the HTML 5 spec. The protocol is still a draft, and only the most recent web browsers support it. However, its benefits are significant enough that we will see the protocol become more popular as more browsers begin to support it. (As always with web development, it's prudent to adhere to the pragmatic strategy of relying on new features when available and falling back on older technology when necessary.)

The WebSocket protocol provides bidirectional communication over a persistent connection between a client and server. The protocol itself uses a new ws:// URL scheme, but is implemented on top of standard HTTP. By using the standard HTTP and HTTPS ports, it avoids all kinds of problems introduced when connecting to sites from networks that sit behind web proxies. The HTML 5 spec not only describes the communication protocol itself, but also the browser APIs that are required to write client-side code that use WebSockets.

Since WebSocket support is already supported in some of the latest browsers and since Tornado helpfully provides a module for it, it's worth seeing how to implement applications that use WebSockets.

Tornado's WebSocket Module

Tornado provides a WebSocketHandler class as part of the websocket module. The class provides hooks for WebSocket events and methods to communicate with the connected client. The open method is called when a new WebSocket connection is opened, and the on_message and on_close methods are called when the connection receives a new message or is closed by the client.

Additionally, the WebSocketHandler class provides the write_message method to send messages to the client and the close method to close the connection. Let's look at a simple handler that repeats the messages it receives back to the client.

```
class EchoHandler(tornado.websocket.WebSocketHandler):
    def on_open(self):
        self.write_message('connected!')

    def on_message(self, message):
        self.write_message(message)
```

As you can see in our EchoHandler implementation, the on_open method simply sends the string "connected!" back to the client using the write_message method provided by the WebSocketHandler base class. The on_message method is invoked every time the handler receives a new message from the client, and our implementation echoes the same message back to the client. That's all there is to it! Let's take a look at a complete example to see how easy this protocol is to implement.

Example: Live Inventory with WebSockets

In this section, we will see how easy it is to update the HTTP long polling example we saw previously to use WebSockets. Keep in mind, however, that WebSockets are a new standard and are only supported by the very latest browser versions. The specific WebSocket protocol versions that Tornado supports are only available in Firefox versions 6.0 and up, Safari 5.0.1, Chrome 6 and higher, and the Internet Explorer 10 developer preview.

With the disclaimer out of the way, let's take a look at the source. Most of the code remains unchanged, but the server application needs a few modifications to the ShoppingCart and StatusHandler classes. Example 5-7 should look familiar.

Example 5-7. Web Sockets: shopping_cart.py

```python
import tornado.web
import tornado.websocket
import tornado.httpserver
import tornado.ioloop
import tornado.options
from uuid import uuid4

class ShoppingCart(object):
    totalInventory = 10
    callbacks = []
    carts = {}

    def register(self, callback):
        self.callbacks.append(callback)

    def unregister(self, callback):
        self.callbacks.remove(callback)

    def moveItemToCart(self, session):
        if session in self.carts:
            return

        self.carts[session] = True
        self.notifyCallbacks()

    def removeItemFromCart(self, session):
        if session not in self.carts:
            return

        del(self.carts[session])
        self.notifyCallbacks()

    def notifyCallbacks(self):
        for callback in self.callbacks:
            callback(self.getInventoryCount())

    def getInventoryCount(self):
        return self.totalInventory - len(self.carts)
```

```python
class DetailHandler(tornado.web.RequestHandler):
    def get(self):
        session = uuid4()
        count = self.application.shoppingCart.getInventoryCount()
        self.render("index.html", session=session, count=count)

class CartHandler(tornado.web.RequestHandler):
    def post(self):
        action = self.get_argument('action')
        session = self.get_argument('session')

        if not session:
            self.set_status(400)
            return

        if action == 'add':
            self.application.shoppingCart.moveItemToCart(session)
        elif action == 'remove':
            self.application.shoppingCart.removeItemFromCart(session)
        else:
            self.set_status(400)

class StatusHandler(tornado.websocket.WebSocketHandler):
    def open(self):
        self.application.shoppingCart.register(self.callback)

    def on_close(self):
        self.application.shoppingCart.unregister(self.callback)

    def on_message(self, message):
        pass

    def callback(self, count):
        self.write_message('{"inventoryCount":"%d"}' % count)

class Application(tornado.web.Application):
    def __init__(self):
        self.shoppingCart = ShoppingCart()

        handlers = [
            (r'/', DetailHandler),
            (r'/cart', CartHandler),
            (r'/cart/status', StatusHandler)
        ]

        settings = {
            'template_path': 'templates',
            'static_path': 'static'
        }

        tornado.web.Application.__init__(self, handlers, **settings)

if __name__ == '__main__':
    tornado.options.parse_command_line()
```

```
app = Application()
server = tornado.httpserver.HTTPServer(app)
server.listen(8000)
tornado.ioloop.IOLoop.instance().start()
```

Other than an additional import statement, we need only to change the ShoppingCart and StatusHandler classes. The first thing to notice is that the tornado.websocket module is required in order to get the WebSocketHandler functionality.

In the ShoppingCart class, we need to make a slight change to the way we notify callbacks. Since WebSockets stay open after a message is sent, we don't need to remove callbacks from the internal list as they are notified. We just iterate over the list and invoke the callbacks with the current inventory count:

```
def notifyCallbacks(self):
    for callback in self.callbacks:
        callback(self.getInventoryCount())
```

The other change is to add the unregister method. The StatusHandler will call this method to remove a callback when a WebSocket connection closes.

```
def unregister(self, callback):
    self.callbacks.remove(callback)
```

The bulk of changes are in the StatusHandler class, which now inherits from tornado.websocket.WebSocketHandler. Instead of implementing handler functions for each of the HTTP methods, WebSocket handlers implement the open and on_message methods, which are called when a connection is opened and when a message is received over the connection, respectively. Additionally, the on_close method is called when a connection is closed by the remote host.

```
class StatusHandler(tornado.websocket.WebSocketHandler):
    def open(self):
        self.application.shoppingCart.register(self.callback)

    def on_close(self):
        self.application.shoppingCart.unregister(self.callback)

    def on_message(self, message):
        pass

    def callback(self, count):
        self.write_message('{"inventoryCount":"%d"}' % count)
```

In our implementation, we register the callback method with the ShoppingCart class when a new connection is opened, and unregister the callback when the connection is closed. Since we're still using the HTTP API calls in the CartHandler class, we don't listen for new messages on the WebSocket connection, so the on_message implementation is empty. (We override the default implementation of on_message to prevent Tornado from raising a NotImplementedError if we happen to receive a message.) Finally, the `callback` method writes the message contents to the WebSocket connection when the inventory changes.

The JavaScript code in this version is virtually identical. We just need to change the `requestInventory` function. Instead of making an AJAX request for the long polling resource, we use the HTML 5 WebSocket API. See Example 5-8.

Example 5-8. Web Sockets: The new requestInventory function from inventory.js

```
function requestInventory() {
    var host = 'ws://localhost:8000/cart/status';

    var websocket = new WebSocket(host);

    websocket.onopen = function (evt) { };
    websocket.onmessage = function(evt) {
        $('#count').html($.parseJSON(evt.data)['inventoryCount']);
    };
    websocket.onerror = function (evt) { };
}
```

After creating a new WebSocket connection to the URL `ws://localhost:8000/cart/status`, we add handler functions for each of the events we want to respond to. The only event we care about in this example is `onmessage`, which updates the contents of the same `count` span that the previous `requestInventory` function modified. (The slight difference is that we have to manually parse the JSON object that the server sent.)

Just as in the previous example, the inventory count is updated dynamically as shoppers add the book to their cart. The difference here is that one persistent WebSocket connection is used instead of re-opening HTTP requests with each long polling update.

The Future of WebSockets

The WebSocket protocol is still in draft form, and may change as it is finalized. However, since the specification has just been submitted to the IETF for final review, it is relatively unlikely to face significant changes. As mentioned in the beginning of this section, the major downside to using the WebSocket protocol right now is that only the very latest browsers support it.

Despite those caveats, WebSockets are a promising new way to implement bidirectional communication between a browser and server. As the protocol gains widespread support, we will start seeing implementations in more prominent applications.

CHAPTER 6

Writing Secure Applications

Very often, secure applications come at the expense of complexity (and developer headaches). The Tornado web server has been designed with a number of security considerations in mind, making it easy to protect against a few well-documented vulnerabilities. Secure cookies prevent a user's local state from being surreptitiously modified by malicious code in his browser. Additionally, browser cookies can be compared with HTTP request parameter values to prevent cross-site request forgery attacks. In this chapter, we will look at features in Tornado that make preventing these attacks easy and then look at a user authentication example that uses these features.

Cookie Vulnerabilities

Many websites use browser cookies to store a user's identity between browser sessions. It's a simple and widely compatible way to store persistent state across browser sessions. Unfortunately, browser cookies are susceptible to a number of well-documented attacks. This section will demonstrate how Tornado prevents a malicious script from tampering with your application's stored cookies.

Cookie Forgery

There are a number of ways cookies can be intercepted in the browser. JavaScript and Flash have read and write access to the cookies on the domain of the page in which they are executed. Browser plug ins also have programmatic access to this data. Cross-site scripting attacks can take advantage of this access to modify the value of a cookie in the visitor's browser.

Secure Cookies

Tornado's secure cookies use a cryptographic signature to verify that the value of a cookie has not been modified by anyone other than the server software. Since a malicious script does not know the secret key, it cannot modify a cookie without the application's knowledge.

Using Secure Cookies

Tornado's `set_secure_cookie()` and `get_secure_cookie()` functions send and retrieve browser cookies that are protected against malicious modifications in the browser. To use these functions, you must specify the `cookie_secret` parameter in the application constructor. Let's look at a simple example.

The application in Example 6-1 will render a page that counts how many times it has been reloaded in the browser. If no cookie has been set (or if the cookie has been tampered with), the application will set a new cookie with the value 1. Otherwise, the application will increment the value read from the cookie.

Example 6-1. Secure Cookie Example: cookie_counter.py

```python
import tornado.httpserver
import tornado.ioloop
import tornado.web
import tornado.options

from tornado.options import define, options
define("port", default=8000, help="run on the given port", type=int)

class MainHandler(tornado.web.RequestHandler):
    def get(self):
        cookie = self.get_secure_cookie("count")
        count = int(cookie) + 1 if cookie else 1

        countString = "1 time" if count == 1 else "%d times" % count

        self.set_secure_cookie("count", str(count))

        self.write(
            '<html><head><title>Cookie Counter</title></head>'
            '<body><h1>You&rsquo;ve viewed this page %s times.</h1>' % countString
            '</body></html>'
        )

if __name__ == "__main__":
    tornado.options.parse_command_line()

    settings = {
        "cookie_secret": "bZJc2sWbQLKos6GkHn/VB9oXwQt8SOROkRvJ5/xJ89E="
    }

    application = tornado.web.Application([
        (r'/', MainHandler)
    ], **settings)

    http_server = tornado.httpserver.HTTPServer(application)
```

```
http_server.listen(options.port)
tornado.ioloop.IOLoop.instance().start()
```

If you inspect the value of the cookie in the browser, you will notice that the value stored for count is MQ==|1310335926|8ef174ecc489ea963c5cdc26ab6d41b49502f2e2. Tornado encodes the cookie value as a Base-64 string and appends a timestamp and an HMAC signature to the cookie contents. If the cookie's timestamp is too old (or from the future), or if the signature doesn't match the expected value, the get_secure_cookie() function assumes the cookie has been tampered with and will return None, as if the cookie had not been set.

> The cookie_secret value passed to the Application constructor should be a unique, random string. Executing the following code snippet in a Python shell will generate one for you:
>
> ```
> >>> import base64, uuid
> >>> base64.b64encode(uuid.uuid4().bytes + uuid.uuid4().bytes)
> 'bZJc2sWbQLKos6GkHn/VB9oXwQt8SOROkRvJ5/xJ89E='
> ```

Tornado's secure cookies are still susceptible to snooping, however. Attackers may be able to intercept cookies via scripts or plug ins in the browser, or simply by eavesdropping unencrypted network data. Remember that cookie values are *signed* rather than *encrypted*. Malicious programs are able to read stored cookies and either transmit their data to arbitrary servers or forge requests by sending them unmodified to the application. Therefore, it's important to avoid storing sensitive user data in a browser cookie.

We also need to be aware of the possibility that a user could modify his own cookies, which could lead to a privilege escalation attack. If, for example, we store the number of remaining articles a user has paid to view in a cookie, we would want to prevent the user from updating that number himself in an attempt to get free content. The httponly and secure cookie properties can help prevent these sorts of attacks.

HTTP-Only and SSL Cookies

Tornado's cookie functionality piggybacks on Python's built-in Cookie module. As such, we can take advantage of some security features it provides. These security attributes are part of the HTTP cookie specification, and instruct the browser on how it may expose the value of the cookie to servers it connects to and scripts that it runs. For example, we could minimize the chances that a cookie's value is intercepted on the network by requiring that it be sent only over an SSL connection. We can also ask that the browser hide the cookie's value from JavaScript.

Setting the secure attribute on a cookie instructs the browser to transfer the cookie only over SSL connections. (It's a little confusing, but this is not the same as Tornado's secure cookies, which are more accurately described as *signed* cookies.) Since Python version 2.6, the Cookie object also supports the httponly attribute. Including this attribute instructs the browser to make the cookie inaccessible to JavaScript, which can prevent cross-site scripting attacks from reading the cookie's value.

To enable these features, you can pass keyword arguments to the `set_cookie` and `set_secure_cookie` methods. For example, a secure, HTTP-only cookie (that's not signed by Tornado) could be sent with the call `self.set_cookie('foo', 'bar', httponly=True, secure=True)`.

Now that we've explored a number of strategies for protecting persistent data stored in cookies, we will look at another common attack vector. "Request Vulnerabilities" on page 96 will look at a way to prevent malicious sites from sending forged requests to your application.

Request Vulnerabilities

One of the main security vulnerabilities facing any web application is the Cross-Site Request Forgery, usually abbreviated CSRF or XSRF, and pronounced "sea surf." This exploit takes advantage of a security hole in the browser that permits a malicious attacker to inject code in a victim site that makes unauthorized requests on behalf of a logged-in user. Let's look at an example.

Anatomy of a Cross-Site Request Forgery

Let's say Alice is a regular customer of Burt's Books. When she's logged into her account on the online store, the website identifies her with a browser cookie. Now suppose an unscrupulous author, Melvin, wants to increase sales of his book. On a web forum that Alice frequents, he has posted an entry with an HTML image tag whose source is a URL that initiates a purchase in the online store. For example:

```
<img src="http://store.burts-books.com/purchase?title=Melvins+Web+Sploitz" />
```

Alice's browser will attempt to fetch the image source and include the legitimate cookies in the request, unaware that instead of a picture of a kitten, the URL initiated a purchase at the online store.

Defending Against Request Forgeries

There are a number of precautions to take in order to prevent this sort of attack. The first requires some forethought on your part when developing your application. Any HTTP requests that cause side effects, like clicking a button to make a purchase, edit account settings, change a password, or delete a document, should use the HTTP POST method. This is good RESTful practice anyway, but it has the additional advantage of preventing trivial XSRF attacks like the malicious image we just saw. However, it doesn't go far enough: a malicious site could still make POST requests to your application through other tactics like HTML forms or the XMLHTTPRequest API. Protecting POST requests requires an additional strategy.

In order to prevent forged POST requests, we will require that each request include as one of its parameters a token that matches a corresponding value stored in a cookie. Our application will provide the token to pages we serve through a cookie header and a hidden HTML form element. When the form on a legitimate page is submitted, it will include the form value as well as the stored cookie. If the two match, our application considers the request valid.

Since third-party sites don't have access to this cookie data, they will be unable to include the token cookie with the request. This effectively prevents untrusted sites from making unauthorized requests. As we'll see, Tornado makes this easy for you, too.

Using Tornado's XSRF protection

You can enable XSRF protection by including the `xsrf_cookies` parameter in the application's constructor:

```
settings = {
    "cookie_secret": "bZJc2sWbQLKos6GkHn/VB9oXwQt8SOROkRvJ5/xJ89E=",
    "xsrf_cookies": True
}

application = tornado.web.Application([
    (r'/', MainHandler),
    (r'/purchase', PurchaseHandler),
], **settings)
```

With this application flag set, Tornado will reject POST, PUT, and DELETE requests that do not contain the correct _xsrf value as a request parameter. Tornado will handle the _xsrf cookies behind the scenes, but you must include the XSRF token in your HTML forms in order to authorize legitimate requests. To do so, simply include a call to the xsrf_form_html function in your template:

```
<form action="/purchase" method="POST">
    {% raw xsrf_form_html() %}
    <input type="text" name="title" />
    <input type="text" name="quantity" />
    <input type="submit" value="Check Out" />
</form>
```

XSRF Tokens and AJAX Requests

AJAX requests also require an _xsrf parameter, but instead of having to explicitly include an _xsrf value when rendering the page, the script is able to query the browser for the value of the cookie on the client side. The following two functions transparently add the token value to AJAX POST requests. The first function fetches a cookie by name, while the second is a convenience function to add the _xsrf parameter to the data object passed to the postJSON function.

```
function getCookie(name) {
    var c = document.cookie.match("\\b" + name + "=([^;]*)\\b");
    return c ? c[1] : undefined;
```

```
    }

    jQuery.postJSON = function(url, data, callback) {
        data._xsrf = getCookie("_xsrf");
        jQuery.ajax({
            url: url,
            data: jQuery.param(data),
            dataType: "json",
            type: "POST",
            success: callback
        });
    }
```

These precautions are a lot to think about, and Tornado's secure cookies support and XSRF protection eases some of the burden on application developers. The built-in security features are helpful, to be sure, but it's important to stay alert when thinking about your application's security. There are a number of online web application security references, and one of the more comprehensive collections of practical countermeasures is Mozilla's Secure Coding Guidelines (*https://wiki.mozilla.org/WebAppSec/Secure_Coding_Guidelines*).

User Authentication

Now that we've seen how to set and retrieve cookies securely and understand the theory behind XSRF attacks, let's look at an example that demonstrates a simple user authentication system. In this section, we will build an application that asks a visitor for her username and stores it in a secure cookie to be retrieved later. Subsequent requests will recognize the returning visitor and display a page customized specifically for her. You'll learn about the login_url parameter and the tornado.web.authenticated decorator, which will eliminate some of the headaches normally involved in such an application.

Example: Welcome Back

In this example, we will simply identify someone by a username stored in a secure cookie. When someone visits our page for the first time in a particular browser (or after her cookie expires), we present a page with a login form. The form is submitted as a POST request that is routed to LoginHandler. The body of the post method calls set_secure_cookie() to store the value submitted in the username request argument.

The Tornado application in Example 6-2 demonstrates the authentication functions we will discuss in this section. The LoginHandler class renders the login form and sets the cookie while the LogoutHandler class deletes it.

Example 6-2. Authenticating visitors: cookies.py

```
import tornado.httpserver
import tornado.ioloop
import tornado.web
```

```
import tornado.options
import os.path

from tornado.options import define, options
define("port", default=8000, help="run on the given port", type=int)

class BaseHandler(tornado.web.RequestHandler):
    def get_current_user(self):
        return self.get_secure_cookie("username")

class LoginHandler(BaseHandler):
    def get(self):
        self.render('login.html')

    def post(self):
        self.set_secure_cookie("username", self.get_argument("username"))
        self.redirect("/")

class WelcomeHandler(BaseHandler):
    @tornado.web.authenticated
    def get(self):
        self.render('index.html', user=self.current_user)

class LogoutHandler(BaseHandler):
    def get(self):
        if (self.get_argument("logout", None)):
            self.clear_cookie("username")
            self.redirect("/")

if __name__ == "__main__":
    tornado.options.parse_command_line()

    settings = {
        "template_path": os.path.join(os.path.dirname(__file__), "templates"),
        "cookie_secret": "bZJc2sWbQLKos6GkHn/VB9oXwQt8SOROkRvJ5/xJ89E=",
        "xsrf_cookies": True,
        "login_url": "/login"
    }

    application = tornado.web.Application([
        (r'/', WelcomeHandler),
        (r'/login', LoginHandler),
        (r'/logout', LogoutHandler)
    ], **settings)

    http_server = tornado.httpserver.HTTPServer(application)
    http_server.listen(options.port)
    tornado.ioloop.IOLoop.instance().start()
```

And the files in Examples 6-3 and 6-4 belong in the application's *templates/* directory.

Example 6-3. Login form: login.html

```
<html>
    <head>
```

```
        <title>Please Log In</title>
    </head>
    <body>
        <form action="/login" method="POST">
            Username: <input type="text" name="username" />
            <input type="submit" value="Log In" />
        </form>
    </body>
</html>
```

Example 6-4. Welcoming returning visitors: index.html

```
<html>
    <head>
        <title>Welcome Back!</title>
    </head>
    <body>
        <h1>Welcome back, {{ user }}</h1>
    </body>
</html>
```

The authenticated Decorator

In order to use Tornado's authentication feature, we need to mark specific handlers as requiring a logged-in user. We can accomplish this using the @tornado.web.authenti cated decorator. When we wrap a handler method with this decorator, Tornado will ensure that the method body will be called only if a valid user is found. Let's take a look at the WelcomeHandler from the example, which renders the *index.html* template only to logged-in users.

```
class WelcomeHandler(BaseHandler):
    @tornado.web.authenticated
    def get(self):
        self.render('index.html', user=self.current_user)
```

Before the get method is called, the authenticated decorator makes sure that the cur rent_user property has a value. (We'll discuss this property shortly.) If the cur rent_user value is considered "falsy" (None, False, 0, or ""), any GET or HEAD requests will redirect the visitor to the URL specified in the login_url application setting. Additionally, a POST request without a valid user will return an HTTP response with a 403 (Forbidden) status.

If a valid user is found, Tornado will invoke the handler method as expected. The authenticated decorator relies on the current_user property and the login_url setting for its full functionality, which we'll look at next.

The current_user property

The request handler class has a current_user property (which is also available to any template the handler renders) that can be used to store the identity of the user authenticated for the current request. By default, its value is None. In order for the authentica ted decorator to successfully identify an authenticated user, you must override the request handler's default get_current_user() method to return the current user.

The actual implementation is up to you, but in this case, we're simply retrieving the visitor's username from a secure cookie. Obviously you'd want to use a more robust technique, but for demonstration purposes, we will use the following method:

```
class BaseHandler(tornado.web.RequestHandler):
    def get_current_user(self):
        return self.get_secure_cookie("username")
```

While the example discussed here doesn't go into storing and retrieving a user's password or other credentials, the techniques described in this chapter can be extended to query a database for credentials with minimal additional effort.

The login_url setting

Let's look at the application constructor briefly. Note that there's a new setting we pass to the application: the login_url is the address of our application's login form. If the get_current_user method returns a falsy value, a handler with the authenticated decorator will redirect the browser to this URL in order to login.

```
settings = {
    "template_path": os.path.join(os.path.dirname(__file__), "templates"),
    "cookie_secret": "bZJc2sWbQLKos6GkHn/VB9oXwQt8SOROkRvJ5/xJ89E=",
    "xsrf_cookies": True,
    "login_url": "/login"
}

application = tornado.web.Application([
    (r'/', WelcomeHandler),
    (r'/login', LoginHandler),
    (r'/logout', LogoutHandler)
], **settings)
```

When Tornado builds the redirect URL, it will also append a next query string parameter, which contains the URL of the resource that initiated the redirect to the log-in page. You can use a line like self.redirect(self.get_argument('next', '/')) to redirect the user back to the referring page after login.

Summing up

We just saw two techniques to help secure your Tornado application as well as an example of how to implement user authentication with the @tornado.web.authentica ted decorator. In Chapter 7, we'll look at how to extend the concepts we've discussed here in an application that authenticates against external web services like Facebook and Twitter.

Authenticating with External Services

The example in Chapter 6 showed how to use secure cookies and the `tornado.web.authenticated` decorator to implement a simple user authentication form. In this chapter, we will look at how to authenticate against third-party services. Popular web APIs like Facebook's and Twitter's use the OAuth protocol to securely verify someone's identity while allowing their users to maintain control over third-party access to their personal information. Tornado offers a number of Python mix-ins that help developers authenticate with external services, either with explicit support for popular services, or through general OAuth support. In this chapter, we'll explore two example applications that use Tornado's `auth` module: one that connects to Twitter and another that connects to Facebook.

The Tornado auth Module

As a web application developer, you might want to allow your users to post updates to Twitter or read recent Facebook statuses directly through your application. Most social network and single sign-on APIs provide a standard workflow for authorizing users on your application. The Tornado `auth` module provides classes for OpenID, OAuth, OAuth 2.0, Twitter, FriendFeed, Google OpenID, the Facebook REST API, and the Facebook Graph API. Although you could implement handlers for a particular external service's authorization process on your own, Tornado's `auth` module provides a simplified workflow for developing applications that connect to any of the supported services.

The Authorization Workflow

The workflow for each of these authentication methods is slightly different, but for the most part, they share the `authorize_redirect` and `get_authenticated_user` methods. The `authorize_redirect` method is used to redirect an unauthenticated user to the external service's authorization page. On the authorization page, the user signs into the service and grants your application access to his account. Typically, you will call the get_authenticated_user method when the user returns to your application with a temporary access code. Calling the get_authenticated_user method exchanges the temporary credentials provided by the authorization redirect process for a set of long-term credentials belonging to the user. The specific authentication classes for Twitter, Facebook, FriendFeed, and Google provide their own functions to make API calls to those services.

Asynchronous Requests

One thing to note about the auth module is its use of Tornado's asynchronous HTTP requests. As we saw in Chapter 5, asynchronous HTTP requests allow the tornado server to handle incoming requests while a pending request is waiting for an outgoing request to return.

We'll take a brief look at how to use asynchronous requests and then dive into an example that uses them. Each handler method that initiates an asynchronous call must be preceded with the @tornado.web.asynchronous decorator.

Example: Sign in With Twitter

Let's walk through an example that uses the Twitter API to authenticate a user. This application will redirect a nonlogged-in user to Twitter's authorization page, which prompts the user for his screenname and password. Twitter then redirects the user to a URL you specify in Twitter's application settings page.

First, you must register a new application on Twitter. The Twitter Developers site (*https://dev.twitter.com/*) has a "Create an app" link where you can get started, if you don't have an app already. Once you create your Twitter application, you will be assigned an access token and a secret that identifies your application to Twitter. You'll need to fill in those values in the appropriate places in the source code we show in this section.

Now let's take a look at the code in Example 7-1.

Example 7-1. View Twitter timeline: twitter.py

```
import tornado.web
import tornado.httpserver
import tornado.auth
import tornado.ioloop

class TwitterHandler(tornado.web.RequestHandler, tornado.auth.TwitterMixin):
    @tornado.web.asynchronous
    def get(self):
        oAuthToken = self.get_secure_cookie('oauth_token')
        oAuthSecret = self.get_secure_cookie('oauth_secret')
        userID = self.get_secure_cookie('user_id')
```

```python
        if self.get_argument('oauth_token', None):
            self.get_authenticated_user(self.async_callback(self._twitter_on_auth))
            return

        elif oAuthToken and oAuthSecret:
            accessToken = {
                'key': oAuthToken,
                'secret': oAuthSecret
            }
            self.twitter_request('/users/show',
                access_token=accessToken,
                user_id=userID,
                callback=self.async_callback(self._twitter_on_user)
            )
            return

        self.authorize_redirect()

    def _twitter_on_auth(self, user):
        if not user:
            self.clear_all_cookies()
            raise tornado.web.HTTPError(500, 'Twitter authentication failed')

        self.set_secure_cookie('user_id', str(user['id']))
        self.set_secure_cookie('oauth_token', user['access_token']['key'])
        self.set_secure_cookie('oauth_secret', user['access_token']['secret'])

        self.redirect('/')

    def _twitter_on_user(self, user):
        if not user:
            self.clear_all_cookies()
            raise tornado.web.HTTPError(500, "Couldn't retrieve user information")

        self.render('home.html', user=user)

class LogoutHandler(tornado.web.RequestHandler):
    def get(self):
        self.clear_all_cookies()
        self.render('logout.html')

class Application(tornado.web.Application):
    def __init__(self):
        handlers = [
            (r'/', TwitterHandler),
            (r'/logout', LogoutHandler)
        ]

        settings = {
            'twitter_consumer_key': 'cWc3 ... d3yg',
            'twitter_consumer_secret': 'nEoT ... cCXB4',
            'cookie_secret': 'NTliOTY5NzJkYTVlMTU0OTAwMTdlNjgzMTA5M2U3OGQ5NDIxZmU3Mg==',
            'template_path': 'templates',
        }
```

```
        tornado.web.Application.__init__(self, handlers, **settings)

if __name__ == '__main__':
    app = Application()
    server = tornado.httpserver.HTTPServer(app)
    server.listen(8000)
    tornado.ioloop.IOLoop.instance().start()
```

The templates in Examples 7-2 and 7-3 should be located in the application's *templates* directory.

Example 7-2. Twitter timeline: home.html

```
<html>
    <head>
        <title>{{ user['name'] }} ({{ user['screen_name'] }}) on Twitter</title>
    </head>

    <body>
        <div>
            <a href="/logout">Sign out</a>
        </div>
        <div>
            <img src="{{ user['profile_image_url'] }}" style="float:left" />
            <h2>About @{{ user['screen_name'] }}</h2>
            <p style="clear:both"><em>{{ user['description'] }}</em></p>
        </div>
        <div>
            <ul>
                <li>{{ user['statuses_count'] }} tweets.</li>
                <li>{{ user['followers_count'] }} followers.</li>
                <li>Following {{ user['friends_count'] }} users.</li>
            </ul>
        </div>
        {% if 'status' in user %}
            <hr />
            <div>
                <p>
                    <strong>{{ user['screen_name'] }}</strong>
                    <em>on {{ ' '.join(user['status']['created_at'].split()[:2]) }}
                        at {{ user['status']['created_at'].split()[3] }}</em>
                </p>
                <p>{{ user['status']['text'] }}</p>
            </div>
        {% end %}
    </body>
</html>
```

Example 7-3. Twitter timeline: logout.html

```
<html>
    <head>
        <title>Tornadoes on Twitter</title>
    </head>
```

```
<body>
    <div>
        <h2>You have successfully signed out.</h2>
        <a href="/">Sign in</a>
    </div>
</body>
</html>
```

Let's break this down piece by piece, starting with the *twitter.py* program. In the Application class's __init__ method, you'll notice two new keys in the settings dictionary: twitter_consumer_key and twitter_consumer_secret. These should be set to the values listed in your Twitter application's detailed settings page. Also note that we're declaring two handlers: a TwitterHandler and a LogoutHandler. Let's turn our attention to those for a minute.

The TwitterHandler class contains the bulk of our application's logic. The two things that are important to immediately note are that the class inherits from tornado.auth.TwitterMixin, which provides the Twitter functionality we will be using in this class, and that the get method is wrapped in the @tornado.web.asynchronous decorator, which we discussed in Chapter 5. Now let's look at the first asynchronous call:

```
if self.get_argument('oauth_token', None):
    self.get_authenticated_user(self.async_callback(self._twitter_on_auth))
    return
```

When a user requests the root resource of our application, we first check to see whether the request includes an oauth_token query string parameter. If so, we treat the request as a callback from Twitter's authorization process.

We then use the auth module's get_authenticated_user method to exchange the temporary token we were given for the user's access token. This method expects a callback parameter, which, in this case, is the self._twitter_on_auth method. The callback is executed when the API request to Twitter returns, and we define it a little further down in our code.

If the oauth_token parameter was not found, we move on and test for the case where we've seen a particular user before.

```
elif oAuthToken and oAuthSecret:
    accessToken = {
        'key': oAuthToken,
        'secret': oAuthSecret
    }
    self.twitter_request('/users/show',
        access_token=accessToken,
        user_id=userID,
        callback=self.async_callback(self._twitter_on_user)
    )
    return
```

This snippet looks for `access_key` and `access_secret` cookies, which our application sets when given a valid user by Twitter. If the values are set, we assemble an access token object with the key and the secret and use the `self.twitter_request` method to make a request to the `/users/show` resource of the Twitter API. Again, you'll notice the asynchronous callback, this time to the `self._twitter_on_user` method that we define later.

The `twitter_request` method expects a resource path as its first parameter, and additionally takes optional keyword arguments for `access_token`, `post_args`, and `callback`. The `access_token` parameter should be a dictionary with keys for `key`, which is the user's OAuth access token, and `secret`, the user's OAuth secret.

If the API call uses the `POST` method, the request arguments should be bundled in a dictionary passed to the `post_args` argument. Query string parameters are specified simply as additional keyword arguments in the method call. In the case of the `/users/show` API call, we are making an HTTP `GET` request, so there is no `post_args` argument, and the required `user_id` API parameter is passed as one of the keyword arguments.

If none of the conditions we discussed above are met, it means the user is visiting our application for the first time (or has logged out or otherwise deleted her cookies) and we want to redirect her to the Twitter authorization page. This is done by calling `self.authorize_redirect()`.

```
def _twitter_on_auth(self, user):
    if not user:
        self.clear_all_cookies()
        raise tornado.web.HTTPError(500, 'Twitter authentication failed')

    self.set_secure_cookie('user_id', str(user['id']))
    self.set_secure_cookie('oauth_token', user['access_token']['key'])
    self.set_secure_cookie('oauth_secret', user['access_token']['secret'])

    self.redirect('/')
```

The callback methods for our Twitter requests are quite straightforward. The `_twitter_on_auth` is called with a `user` parameter, which is a dictionary of user data for the authorized user. Our method implementation simply checks that we received a valid user and if so, sets the appropriate cookies. Once the cookies are set, we redirect the user to the root resource, which makes the request to the `/users/show` API method as discussed earlier.

```
def _twitter_on_user(self, user):
    if not user:
        self.clear_all_cookies()
        raise tornado.web.HTTPError(500, "Couldn't retrieve user information")

    self.render('home.html', user=user)
```

The `_twitter_on_user` method is the callback we specified in the call to the `twitter_request` method. When Twitter responds with the user's profile information, our callback renders the *home.html* template with data from the response. The template displays the user's profile image, screenname, and description, as well as some statistics about friend and follower counts and the user's most recent status update.

The `LogoutHandler` method simply clears any stored cookies we stored for a user of the application. It renders the *logout.html* template to provide feedback to the user and allow him to sign in again by redirecting to Twitter. That's all there is to it!

The Twitter application we just looked at simply displays user info for an authenticated user, but it demonstrates how Tornado's `auth` module makes developing social applications much easier. Building an application that can post to a user's Twitter stream is left as an exercise for the reader.

Example: Facebook Authentication and the Graph API

The Facebook example is structurally very similar to the Twitter example we just saw. Facebook has two different API standards, the original REST API and the Facebook Graph API. While both are currently supported, the Graph API is the recommended way to develop new Facebook applications. Tornado supports both APIs in the `auth` module, but we will focus on the Graph API in this example.

In order to prepare for this example, you will need to sign in to Facebook's developer site (*http://developers.facebook.com/*) and create a new application. You will be asked to name your application and asked to prove you are not a robot. In order to authorize users from your own domain, you will need to specify your application's domain name. Then click the "Website" box under the "Select how your app integrates with Facebook" heading. You will need to enter your site's URL here as well. For a more complete guide to setting up a Facebook app, the developer guides are a good start: *https://devel opers.facebook.com/docs/guides/web/*.

Once your application is set up, you will use the application ID and secret provided in the Basic Settings page to connect to the Facebook Graph API.

Recall from the previous section that the single sign-on workflow will direct a user to the Facebook platform to authorize the application, and Facebook will use an HTTP redirect to send the user back to your server with an authorization code. Once you receive the request with the code, you must request the authorization token which is used to identify the user making the API requests.

This example app will render the user's timeline and allow the user to update her Facebook status though our interface. Let's take a look at Example 7-4.

Example 7-4. Facebook Authentication: facebook.py

```
import tornado.web
import tornado.httpserver
import tornado.auth
import tornado.ioloop
import tornado.options
from datetime import datetime
```

```python
class FeedHandler(tornado.web.RequestHandler, tornado.auth.FacebookGraphMixin):
    @tornado.web.asynchronous
    def get(self):
        accessToken = self.get_secure_cookie('access_token')
        if not accessToken:
            self.redirect('/auth/login')
            return

        self.facebook_request(
            "/me/feed",
            access_token=accessToken,
            callback=self.async_callback(self._on_facebook_user_feed))

    def _on_facebook_user_feed(self, response):
        name = self.get_secure_cookie('user_name')
        self.render('home.html', feed=response['data'] if response else [], name=name)

    @tornado.web.asynchronous
    def post(self):
        accessToken = self.get_secure_cookie('access_token')
        if not accessToken:
            self.redirect('/auth/login')

        userInput = self.get_argument('message')

        self.facebook_request(
            "/me/feed",
            post_args={'message': userInput},
            access_token=accessToken,
            callback=self.async_callback(self._on_facebook_post_status))

    def _on_facebook_post_status(self, response):
        self.redirect('/')

class LoginHandler(tornado.web.RequestHandler, tornado.auth.FacebookGraphMixin):
    @tornado.web.asynchronous
    def get(self):
        userID = self.get_secure_cookie('user_id')

        if self.get_argument('code', None):
            self.get_authenticated_user(
                redirect_uri='http://example.com/auth/login',
                client_id=self.settings['facebook_api_key'],
                client_secret=self.settings['facebook_secret'],
                code=self.get_argument('code'),
                callback=self.async_callback(self._on_facebook_login))
            return
        elif self.get_secure_cookie('access_token'):
            self.redirect('/')
            return

        self.authorize_redirect(
            redirect_uri='http://example.com/auth/login',
            client_id=self.settings['facebook_api_key'],
```

```
                extra_params={'scope': 'read_stream,publish_stream'}
            )

    def _on_facebook_login(self, user):
        if not user:
            self.clear_all_cookies()
            raise tornado.web.HTTPError(500, 'Facebook authentication failed')

        self.set_secure_cookie('user_id', str(user['id']))
        self.set_secure_cookie('user_name', str(user['name']))
        self.set_secure_cookie('access_token', str(user['access_token']))
        self.redirect('/')

class LogoutHandler(tornado.web.RequestHandler):
    def get(self):
        self.clear_all_cookies()
        self.render('logout.html')

class FeedListItem(tornado.web.UIModule):
    def render(self, statusItem):
        dateFormatter = lambda x: datetime.
strptime(x,'%Y-%m-%dT%H:%M:%S+0000').strftime('%c')
        return self.render_string('entry.html', item=statusItem, format=dateFormatter)

class Application(tornado.web.Application):
    def __init__(self):
        handlers = [
            (r'/', FeedHandler),
            (r'/auth/login', LoginHandler),
            (r'/auth/logout', LogoutHandler)
        ]

        settings = {
            'facebook_api_key': '2040 ... 8759',
            'facebook_secret': 'eae0 ... 2f08',
            'cookie_secret': 'NTliOTY5NzJkYTVlMTU0OTAwMTdlNjgzMTA5M2U3OGQ5NDIxZmU3Mg==',
            'template_path': 'templates',
            'ui_modules': {'FeedListItem': FeedListItem}
        }

        tornado.web.Application.__init__(self, handlers, **settings)

if __name__ == '__main__':
    tornado.options.parse_command_line()

    app = Application()
    server = tornado.httpserver.HTTPServer(app)
    server.listen(8000)
    tornado.ioloop.IOLoop.instance().start()
```

We'll walk through the handlers in the order that a visitor would interact with them. When the root URL is requested, the FeedHandler will look for the access_token cookie. If the cookie is not present, the user will be directed to the *auth/login* URL.

The login page uses the `authorize_redirect` method to redirect the user to Facebook's authorization dialog box, where the user will login to Facebook if required, review the permissions the application is requesting, and approve the application. Upon clicking "Approve," she will be directed back to the application, to the URL specified in the `redirect_uri` parameter given in the call to `authorize_redirect`.

When returning from the Facebook authorization screen, the request to */auth/login* will include a `code` parameter as a query-string argument. This code is a temporary token that is exchanged for more permanent credentials. If the `code` argument is found, the application will make a Facebook Graph API request to retrieve the authenticated user and store her user ID, full name, and the access token that will identify her when the application makes Graph API calls.

Once these values have been stored, the user is directed back to the root URL. Upon returning to the root page, the user will this time get a listing of recent Facebook feed messages. The application sees that an `access_token` cookie is set and uses the `facebook_request` method to query the Graph API for the user's feed. We pass the OAuth token to the `facebook_request` method, which also takes a callback argument—in Example 7-5, it is the `_on_facebook_user_feed` method.

Example 7-5. Facebook Authentication: home.html

```
<html>
    <head>
        <title>{{ name }} on Facebook</title>
    </head>

    <body>
        <div>
            <a href="/auth/logout">Sign out</a>
            <h1>{{ name }}</h1>
        </div>
        <div>
            <form action="/facebook/" method="POST">
                <textarea rows="3" cols="50" name="message"></textarea>
                <input type="submit" value="Update Status" />
            </form>
        </div>
        <hr />
        {% for item in feed %}
            {% module FeedListItem(item) %}
        {% end %}
    </body>
</html>
```

When the callback is invoked with the user's feed response from Facebook, the application renders the *home.html* template, which uses the `FeedListItem` UI module to render each of the entries in the list. At the top of the template, we render a form that posts to the */* resource on our server with a `message` parameter. The application forwards this call to the Graph API to post an update.

To post the update, we use the `facebook_request` method again. This time, in addition to the `access_token` parameter, we include a `post_args` parameter with a dictionary of arguments that become the post body for the Graph request. When this call succeeds, we redirect the user back to the home page, which requests the updated timeline once again.

As you can see, the Facebook authentication classes in Tornado's `auth` module provide a number of helpful features for building Facebook applications. This is a great asset for rapid prototyping, but it also holds up well in production applications.

CHAPTER 8

Deploying Tornado

Until now, we've been running only single Tornado processes in our examples for simplicity's sake. It made testing an application and making quick changes extremely easy, but it is not an appropriate deployment strategy. Deploying an application to a production environment presents new challenges, with both maximizing performance and managing the individual processes. This chapter presents strategies to harden your Tornado application and increase request throughput, as well as tools that make deploying Tornado servers easier.

Reasons for Running Multiple Tornado Instances

In most cases, assembling a web page is not a particularly computationally intensive process. The server needs to parse the request, fetch the appropriate data, and assemble the various components that make up the response. If your application makes blocking calls to query a database or access the filesystem, the server will not be able to respond to an incoming request while it is waiting for the call to complete. In these moments, the server hardware will have surplus CPU time while it waits for I/O operations to complete.

Given that most of the elapsed time responding to an HTTP request is spent with the CPU idle, we'd like to take advantage of this downtime and maximize the number of requests we can handle at a given time. That is, we'd like the server to be able to accept as many new requests as possible while the processes handling open requests are waiting for data.

As we saw in Chapter 5, when we discussed asynchronous HTTP requests, Tornado's nonblocking architecture goes a long way towards solving this problem for us. Recall that the asynchronous requests allow a Tornado process to fulfill incoming requests while waiting for an outbound request to return. The problem we run into, however, is when synchronous function calls block. If a database query or disk access blocks the Tornado process, that process is barred from answering new requests. The easiest way around this problem is to run multiple instances of the interpreter. Typically, you would want to use a reverse proxy like Nginx to distribute load across multiple Tornado instances.

Using Nginx as a Reverse Proxy

A proxy server is a machine that relays a client's resource request to the appropriate server. Some network installations use proxy servers to filter and cache HTTP requests that machines on the local network make to the Internet. Since we will be running a number of Tornado instances on a range of TCP ports, we will use a proxy server in reverse: clients across the Internet will connect to a reverse proxy server, which will forward requests to any one host in a pool of Tornado servers behind the proxy. The proxy server is designed to be transparent to the client and yet pass valuable information like the original client's IP address and TCP scheme to the upstream Tornado node.

Our server configuration is illustrated in Figure 8-1. The reverse proxy receives all incoming HTTP requests and distributes them evenly among the individual Tornado instances.

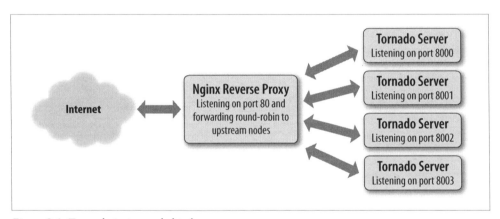

Figure 8-1. Tornado instances behind a reverse proxy server

Basic Nginx Configuration

The listing in Example 8-1 is an example Nginx configuration. This Nginx setup listens for connections on port 80 and distributes those requests among the upstream hosts listed in the configuration file. In this case, we will assume the upstream hosts are listening for connections on their own port on the loopback interface.

Example 8-1. A bare-bones Nginx proxy configuration

```
user nginx;
worker_processes 5;

error_log /var/log/nginx/error.log;
```

```
pid /var/run/nginx.pid;

events {
    worker_connections 1024;
    use epoll;
}

proxy_next_upstream error;

upstream tornadoes {
    server 127.0.0.1:8000;
    server 127.0.0.1:8001;
    server 127.0.0.1:8002;
    server 127.0.0.1:8003;
}

server {
    listen 80;
    server_name www.example.org *.example.org;

    location /static/ {
        root /var/www/static;
        if ($query_string) {
            expires max;
        }
    }

    location / {
        proxy_pass_header Server;
        proxy_set_header Host $http_host;
        proxy_redirect off;
        proxy_set_header X-Real-IP $remote_addr;
        proxy_set_header X-Scheme $scheme;
        proxy_pass http://tornadoes;
    }
}
```

 This configuration example assumes your system uses *epoll*. There are often subtle differences between UNIX flavors. Some systems may use *poll*, */dev/poll*, or *kqueue* instead.

It may be helpful to walk through the order that requests are matched to either `location /static/` or `location /`. Nginx treats a literal string in the location directive as if it were a regular expression that starts with a beginning-of-line anchor and ends with any repetition of any characters. So / is treated as the expression ^/.*. When Nginx matches against literal strings, more specific strings like **/static/** are checked against the request URL before more general strings like /. The Nginx documentation explains the matching order in greater detail.

Aside from some of the standard boilerplate, the important parts of this configuration file are the `upstream` directive and the proxy directives in the server configuration. The Nginx server listens for connections on port 80 and distributes those requests among the Tornado instances listed in the `upstream` server group. The `proxy_pass` directive specifies the URI of the server that is accepting forwarded requests. You can reference an `upstream` server group by name in the host portion of the `proxy_pass` URI.

Nginx will by default distribute requests in a simple round-robin fashion. Alternatively, you can choose to distribute requests based on the client's IP address, which (barring connection interruptions) will guarantee that requests originating from the same IP address will always be routed to the same upstream node. You can read more about this option in the `HTTPUpstreamModule` documentation. (*http://wiki.nginx.org/HttpUp streamModule*)

Also note the `location /static/` directive, which tells Nginx to serve files in the static directory directly instead of proxying the requests to Tornado. Nginx can serve static files much more efficiently than Tornado, so it makes sense to keep the unnecessary load off the Tornado processes.

SSL Decryption with Nginx

Developers of applications that transfer personal information between the browser and client need to take special care to protect that information from falling into the wrong hands. With unsecured WiFi access as common as it is, users are susceptible to cookie hijacking attacks that compromise their accounts on popular social networking sites. In response, most major social web applications have made their sites either use encrypted protocols by default or as a user-configurable option. Coincidentally, we can use for Nginx to decrypt SSL encryption on incoming requests and distribute the decoded HTTP requests to the upstream servers.

Example 8-2 shows a `server` block that decrypts incoming HTTPS requests and forwards the decrypted traffic using the proxy directives we saw in Example 8-1.

Example 8-2. server block using SSL

```
server {
    listen 443;
    ssl on;
    ssl_certificate /path/to/cert.pem;
    ssl_certificate_key /path/to/cert.key;

    default_type application/octet-stream;

    location /static/ {
        root /var/www/static;
        if ($query_string) {
            expires max;
        }
    }

    location = /favicon.ico {
        rewrite (.*) /static/favicon.ico;
    }
```

```
    location / {
        proxy_pass_header Server;
        proxy_set_header Host $http_host;
        proxy_redirect off;
        proxy_set_header X-Real-IP $remote_addr;
        proxy_set_header X-Scheme $scheme;
        proxy_pass http://tornadoes;
    }
}
```

This works exactly like the previous configuration, with the exception that Nginx will be listening for secure web requests on the standard HTTPS port 443. If you want to enforce an SSL connection, you can include a rewrite directive in the **server** block that listens for HTTP connections on port 80. See Example 8-3 for an example of that redirect.

Example 8-3. server block to redirect HTTP requests to a secure channel

```
server {
    listen 80;
    server_name example.com;

    rewrite /(.*) https://$http_host/$1 redirect;
}
```

Nginx is a very robust tool, and we've barely scratched the surface of the possible configuration options that can be helpful for Tornado deployments. The Nginx documentation wiki (*http://wiki.nginx.org/*) is an excellent resource for additional information on installing and configuring this powerful software.

Using Supervisor to Manage Tornado Processes

As we foreshadowed in "Using Nginx as a Reverse Proxy" on page 116, we will be running many instances of our Tornado application to take advantage of modern multiprocessor and multicore server architecture. Most anecdotal reports from deployment teams recommend running one Tornado process per core. As we know, however, the plural of anecdote is not data, so your results may vary. In this section, we will discuss strategies for managing many Tornado instances on a UNIX system.

So far, we've run the Tornado server from the command line with a command like $ **python main.py --port=8000**. In long-term production deployments however, this is unmanageable. Because we are running a separate Tornado process for each CPU core, there are several processes to monitor and control. The *supervisor* daemon can help us with this task.

Supervisor is designed to launch at boot time and start the processes listed in its configuration file. Here, we will look at Supervisor configuration to manage the four Tornado instances we referenced as upstream hosts in our Nginx configuration. Typically *supervisord.conf* contains global configuration directives, and will load additional configuration files from a *conf.d* directory. Example 8-4 shows a configuration file for the Tornado processes we want to start.

Example 8-4. tornado.conf

```
[group:tornadoes]
programs=tornado-8000,tornado-8001,tornado-8002,tornado-8003

[program:tornado-8000]
command=python /var/www/main.py --port=8000
directory=/var/www
user=www-data
autorestart=true
redirect_stderr=true
stdout_logfile=/var/log/tornado.log
loglevel=info

[program:tornado-8001]
command=python /var/www/main.py --port=8001
directory=/var/www
user=www-data
autorestart=true
redirect_stderr=true
stdout_logfile=/var/log/tornado.log
loglevel=info

[program:tornado-8002]
command=python /var/www/main.py --port=8002
directory=/var/www
user=www-data
autorestart=true
redirect_stderr=true
stdout_logfile=/var/log/tornado.log
loglevel=info

[program:tornado-8003]
command=python /var/www/main.py --port=8003
directory=/var/www
user=www-data
autorestart=true
redirect_stderr=true
stdout_logfile=/var/log/tornado.log
loglevel=info
```

In order for Supervisor to do anything useful, you will need at least one `program` section. In Example 8-4, we've declared four programs, named `tornado-8000` through `tornado-8003`. The program sections define the parameters for the individual command that Supervisor will run. A value for `command` is required, which will typically be the Tornado application with the `port` argument that we want to listen on. We also define additional settings for the program's working directory, effective user, and logfile; and it's helpful to set the `autorestart` and `redirect_stderr` settings to `true`.

In order to manage all the Tornado processes in aggregate, it's helpful to create a group. At the top of our example, we declare a group called tornadoes and list the individual programs that make up that group. Now, when we want to manage our Tornado app, we can reference all the constituent programs by the group name followed by the wildcard character. To restart the app, for example, we would issue the command restart tornadoes:* in the *supervisorctl* utility.

Once you've installed and configured Supervisor, you can use *supervisorctl* to manage the *supervisord* process. To start your web application, you can instruct Supervisor to reread its configuration, and any programs or program groups whose configuration has changed will be restarted. You can also manually start, stop, and restart managed programs or check the overall system status.

```
supervisor> update
tornadoes: stopped
tornadoes: updated process group
supervisor> status
tornadoes:tornado-8000           RUNNING     pid 32091, uptime 00:00:02
tornadoes:tornado-8001           RUNNING     pid 32092, uptime 00:00:02
tornadoes:tornado-8002           RUNNING     pid 32093, uptime 00:00:02
tornadoes:tornado-8003           RUNNING     pid 32094, uptime 00:00:02
```

Supervisor works with your system's init process, and it should automatically register the daemon to launch at boot time. Program groups automatically come online when *supervisor* starts up. By default, Supervisor will monitor the child processes and respawn any individual program that unexpectedly terminates. If you want to restart managed processes without regard to their exit codes, you can set the autorestart to true.

Not only does Supervisor make managing many Tornado instances easier, it also provides some peace of mind that your Tornado servers will come back online after an unexpected service interruption.

About the Authors

Michael Dory has spent the last decade studying the ways people communicate, and working to make their conversations better. As the co-founder and CTO of the social technology agency Socialbomb, he's worked with brands, agencies, and startups to build social applications and platforms that connect users with their friends, their devices, and the world around them.

Adam Parrish is an artist and programmer, currently residing in Brooklyn. He has 10 years of professional programming experience, with an emphasis on programming for the Web.

Brendan Berg has over five years of professional experience developing web and mobile applications. Previously, he developed mobile applications, cloud infrastructure, and APIs as Chief Software Architect at Socialbomb. Now he's focusing on creating software for the freelance ecosystem as the co-founder and CTO of Wurk Happy.

Get even more for your money.

Join the O'Reilly Community, and register the O'Reilly books you own. It's free, and you'll get:

- $4.99 ebook upgrade offer
- 40% upgrade offer on O'Reilly print books
- Membership discounts on books and events
- Free lifetime updates to ebooks and videos
- Multiple ebook formats, DRM FREE
- Participation in the O'Reilly community
- Newsletters
- Account management
- 100% Satisfaction Guarantee

Signing up is easy:

1. **Go to: oreilly.com/go/register**
2. **Create an O'Reilly login.**
3. **Provide your address.**
4. **Register your books.**

Note: English-language books only

To order books online:
oreilly.com/store

For questions about products or an order:
orders@oreilly.com

To sign up to get topic-specific email announcements and/or news about upcoming books, conferences, special offers, and new technologies:
elists@oreilly.com

For technical questions about book content:
booktech@oreilly.com

To submit new book proposals to our editors:
proposals@oreilly.com

O'Reilly books are available in multiple DRM-free ebook formats. For more information:
oreilly.com/ebooks

O'REILLY®

Spreading the knowledge of innovators   oreilly.com

Have it your way.

Made in the USA
San Bernardino, CA
19 April 2013